101 Portrait photography tips

For amateur photographers

document.

Steve Pease

Introduction

This book is written to help regular people learn to take portraits like a pro. There are according to estimates close to two billion photos taken every day. Most of them are snapshots. Almost everyone has a camera on them all the time with modern cell phones.

Many of these photos taken are shots of people, friends, and family. Most of the photos taken are a quick shot with no planning or composition. They are shots people want to take to remember something important to them, a moment in time. Most of the shots are capturing an image of what they want to see. However, they are not shots most people would say are great.

If you use the tips in this book, you can take your photos from ok to great. Your everyday photos will be excellent enough to make prints. And some of them will be shots who others will say WOW when they see them and will want copies.

I have taken several hundred thousand pictures over the last 35 years, and I am constantly trying to improve my photography. My goal is always to take the best shots I can. I want people to say wow when they look at my shots.

I went through the photography course at New York Institute of photography many years ago. What I learned from the course, and my years of experience were worth every dollar. The key to be a great photographer is to see things that most people do not see, or in a way, they did not see it.

My favorite types of photography are landscape, portrait, animals, black and white, and infrared. I have shot several weddings and spend hundreds of hours just exploring different places looking for great things to take pictures of.

Portrait photography is fun because you not only have to compose the shot, but you also must pose the subject to get the composition right. With other types of photography, the subject is an inanimate object. It could be a mountain or a building or any number of other objects. If it is wildlife, you take what you can get at the time.

Posing the subject can be a challenge or fun. If you make it fun, it will make your photography easier, and you will be a better portrait photographer. To pose the subject, you need to know what looks good for the subject you are shooting. It also matters what the shot is to be used for. A sexy shot of a model, compared to a shot of a person for a business newsletter, are completely different.

If you use Evernote, set up a series of swipe files that you can access anywhere. As you are surfing the web and books or magazines, and you see portraits that you like. Save them in your swipe files so you can use them for reference in the future. Then when you are looking for a good pose or type of shot, you have it there to re-create, or pose a similar look.

I have an Evernote folder for each type of portrait shot. A file for women for all types of situations. A file for men, kids, babies, groups, seniors, pets, etc. Any type of portraits you will be shooting. I keep headshots, half body and full body shots. If you have this, you can plan before the shoot, so you know what you want to do. Adlibbing can work but having a plan will work better.

If you don't use **Evernote,** you should. They have a free version that will let you store your swipe files to use on any device. You can use any other file storage program the same way. Set these files up, it will help you a lot when you want to shoot portraits.

One more very cool thing online that you can use is Google Photo Storage. You can store an unlimited number of good-quality resolution shot, for no charge. I have over 300,000 photos stored on their server. I still save my originals at least two other ways, but this is awesome. I store mine at full resolution. When you use up your space, it costs you a little to store them, but it is very reasonable.

Not only do you get free storage. The site sorts your shot for you. I can look at the people section and click on a picture of my wife. The software will pull up almost every shot I have of her in a couple of seconds. This makes storing your photos quite easy and being able to access the ones you want when you want to see them.

If you have any questions or comments. Contact me at mailto:steve@stevepease.net or visit stevepease.net for more great books.

Table of Contents

Equipment

Camera

Type of Camera needed

It is preferable to use an SLR when taking portraits. There are big advantages to having total control. Having control of the aperture, shutter speed and ISO, is great. However, you can still take some fantastic shots without a DSLR.

One of the keys to getting great portrait shots without an SLR is to get in close to the subject. What this does is allows you to fill the screen with the subject. Then blur the background to give better isolation for the subject, with no distraction from the background.

Many people now take most of their pictures from a phone camera, including portraits. The iPhone seven plus and newer models have a great portrait mode on them. It uses both camera lenses and blurs the background for you. It works well and takes great shots.

Be careful when you edit your phone photos that you do not over edit them. Many apps on the market give you lots of filters to make major changes to the photo. There are four apps that I use when I edit phone photos for different things. They are, be funky, enlight, Snap seed, and Pics Play.

Each of these apps has different filters I like. They each give you options for quick changes. They also give you control to not over edit and make the photos look fake.

SOME GENERAL TIPS

When taking phone portraits, try to find a reflective surface to use in the photo to add interest to your shot, if you are not filling the frame with the subject. A reflective surface in front of the subject can add a lot of interest to the photo while not detracting from it. Even something like a shiny table or counter can work well.

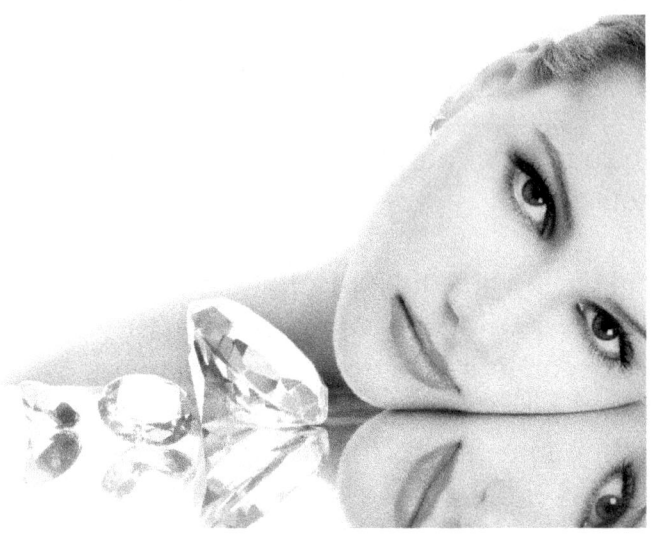

Taking the portrait through a window, reflecting something interesting outside. Things like trees, or a mountain or any other interesting object, can make a cool portrait. You can even use the window for interest with reflection of the subject.

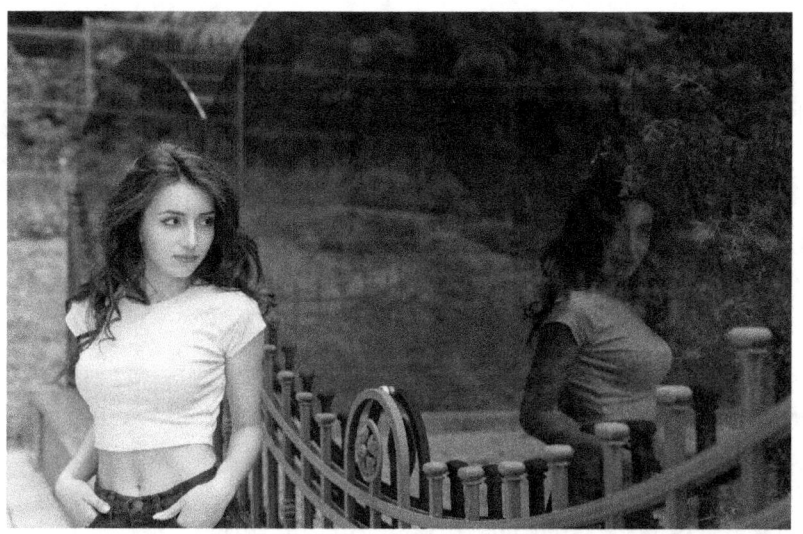

Turn on the grid in your phone so you can use the rule of thirds to compose your photos.

Do not use your digital zoom on your camera unless you must. Try to move closer to the subject so you do not lose resolution in the picture. Sometimes it is impossible, there are obstacles preventing you from getting nearer to the subject. Things like water or other things that prevent you from getting in for a tighter shot. Only use the digital zoom as a last resort.

Camera settings

There are five camera settings that are important in photography. Those settings can make a big difference in your portraits. If you are not using an SLR, set your camera to the portrait mode. This mode will make the camera try to give you the optimal setting to get the best portraits.

If you have an SLR, use the settings below.

Mode setting

The best setting to use for portraits is aperture priority. Aperture priority gives you the most control of depth of field. Depth of field is important in portrait shooting. Controlling depth of field gives you total power over the background, and if it is out of focus or not. The camera will set the shutter speed from the aperture you choose. It regulates the amount of light coming through the lens.

You can also set it to the manual mode. Manual lets you control both aperture and shutter speed. I do this sometimes if I am going for a different look, like a high key shot or a low-key shot. Otherwise most modern cameras have incredibly good sensors for setting the shutter speed.

I also prefer to shoot in raw mode. Raw mode stops the camera from processing the photo to what it thinks you want. It lets you do it after you get the shot. Many of the photos I take would be fine if processed in Jpeg, so I set my camera to shoot a raw and jpeg. It takes more space on the card. It also takes more time post processing. However, if you get a great shot that needs some adjusting, raw mode lets you fix it a lot easier.

I prefer shooting in natural light. Sometimes you need to make some adjustments. Those few great photos that you can fix, make it worth shooting in raw mode.

Focus setting.

Single shot autofocus will work best for most situations. One thing you need to know and be careful of is the focus point. In my camera, I can set the focus point in the shot to one of 10 points. Where you focus in a portrait shot is critical. I normally set it for the center spot. I set the focus and the metering for where I want it in the center of the frame. Hold the shutter button down halfway, compose the shot, and make the photo.

Exposure

The exposure settings can vary a bit from camera to camera. I tend to like a darker than lighter look to my photos. It looks better, and it is easier to fix somewhat underexposed than it is to fix photos that are over exposed.

White Balance

White Balance also will work well on auto most of the time. If there is a problem, you can fix it in the post processing if you shoot in raw mode.

ISO

For most situations set the ISO at 100. This setting will give you the crispest cleanest shots. If shooting in low light, you can use the ISO to allow additional light through the lens. This lets you get the shutter speed faster, so the shots are not blurred.

Know your camera and know where the noise gets beyond the point where it is noticeable. Do not set the ISO higher than that. Most are around 800 to 1600 ISO with DSLRs. That point is normally lower with point and shoot cameras. The bigger the sensor, the lower the noise, for the most part. Full-frame cameras are best but are much more expensive. I do not shoot portraits above 400 ISO most of the time. You want portraits to be sharp and crisp.

Aperture

Set the aperture for f1.8 to f8. This will let you control the background blur. If you are shooting a group, you need to set the aperture to f5.6 or even f8 to get everyone in focus. The smaller the number, the more the background will be blurred.

Shutter speed

The shutter speed will be set by the camera when using aperture priority. You want to keep it in the 1/60 to 1/250, depending on if there is any movement by the subject. When taking candid photos, especially of kids, set the shutter speed a bit higher, they tend to move a lot.

These settings are all guidelines that give a place to start and to use in most situations. I many times go outside of these settings when the situation dictates. There are always exceptions. Especially when you are trying to do something a bit different.

Experiment with the different settings to see what works for your unique portraits.

Lenses

The best portrait lenses are 75mm to 125mm. Remember that with a digital camera, the focal length of the lens is longer than what is on the lens. Most of the time by about ½ times longer. A 50mm f1.8 lens makes a great portrait lens for most portrait shoots at close range. On a digital SLR, a 50mm lens is a 75mm lens. On a full-frame camera, a 50mm lens will give you a fisheye type of look. This is not flattering for portraits.

A 100mm macro lens is also an exceptionally good portrait lens.

A decent 75mm to 300mm is a great portrait lens as well in the 75mm range. It is the right focal length at about 105mm. It is also perfect when you are taking candid shots. You can zoom out and catch great shots that would not be as good with a shorter lens. Zooming for longer range shots will also blur the background for you.

Flash

I like to use natural light as much as I can. I also like to use constant lights in some situations. Because they are simple to set up, and you can change locations fast and easy.

If I do use flash, I use it as fill flash when a reflector will not suffice. If I am shooting in a studio setting or indoors where I am not going to be moving the location. I can get better more real looking portrait shots with natural light and a reflector or two. Or I use an umbrella to reflect the light back on the subject to defuse it.

Reflector

If you do not have a photographer's reflector, a great substitute is one or two foam craft boards that are 2ft by 3ft. You can use different color reflectors. This will give the subject a distinctive look. Gold and silver get used often although I prefer white for most set ups.

Use a photographer's reflector. A white one lets the sunshine through it and will work as a diffuser for harsh sunlight. Direct sunlight is terrible for portraits. You will create your own shade with a diffuser.

When you are setting up a shot, get the reflectors in position without even looking through the lens. Look at the subjects face and move the diffuser around, so you fill in all the dark shadows of their face. When you look through the lens, you should see the same lighting.

It is nice to have an assistant when you are using reflectors or a diffuser. You need something to hold the diffuser. A tripod with a clamp will work, but an assistant is nice, they can move it around quickly as needed.

Tripod

If you are shooting in a studio. A tripod gives you a huge advantage. If you are shooting an outdoor setting, or capturing candid portraits, a tripod does not work well. Most photographers will tell you to use a tripod. It is a good idea, but I spend most of my time shooting portraits in situations when it does not work well.

You will need to determine in each situation if it is a good idea. Use one when you can, you will get sharper shots.

Here is a great shot using many of the best ideas for fantastic portraits. And it is like I said I like shots, a bit darker.

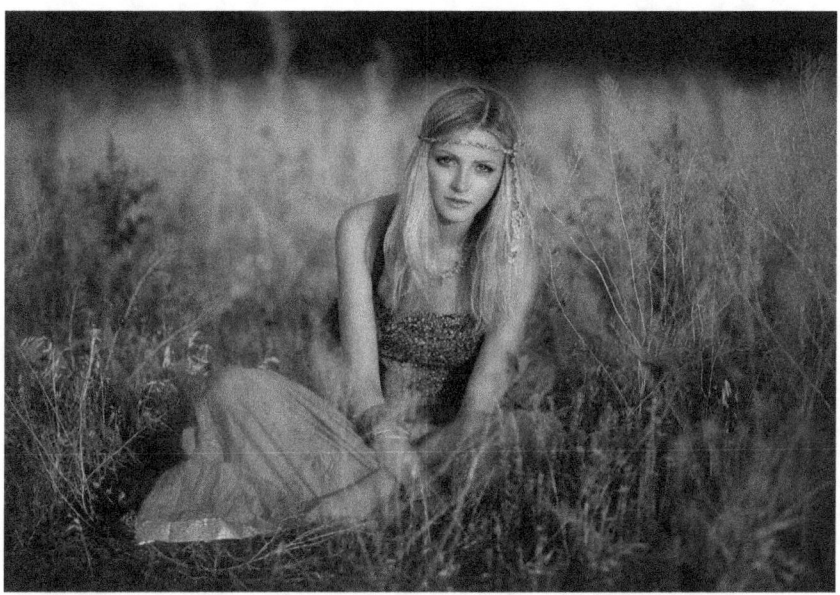

Even though she is almost in the center of the shot, I think it works well for many reasons. The background is blurred enough to focus the attention on the subject. Her face is sharp and clear; the lighting is natural and just the right intensity to capture who she is.

Composition

"Photography for me is not looking; it's feeling. If you cannot feel what you are looking at, then you're never going to get others to feel anything when they look at your pictures."

— Don McCullin

The 2 most important parts of a great portrait are lighting and composition. To make an excellent portrait, you need to merge the two parts together to make it all work.

Great composition is doable in a couple of ways. In portraiture many times, all you must do is to fill the whole frame with the subject, or even part of the subject. By doing this you can clear out anything else from taking away from the subject.

You must focus the viewer's' attention about the portrait. And sometimes add things to enhance the subject.

There are four basic composition set ups for taking portrait. The first is to fill the frame with the subject; this is generally a headshot or a face shot.

The second is a photo from the chest up. The third is a full body shot. The fourth is a full body picture with props or interesting background objects.

In the full frame shot, you want to get the perfect expression and the best part of the face to capture the finest image.

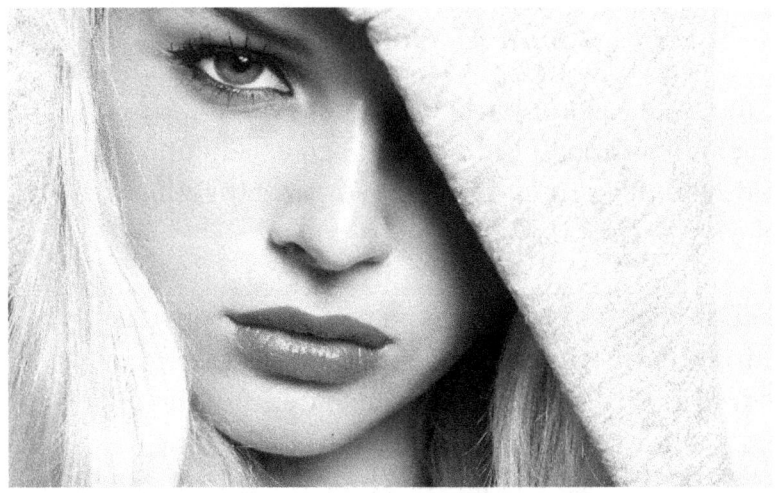

In a chest up photo, you will want to focus on getting the subject's best side. Or getting their finest features as the focus of the shot.

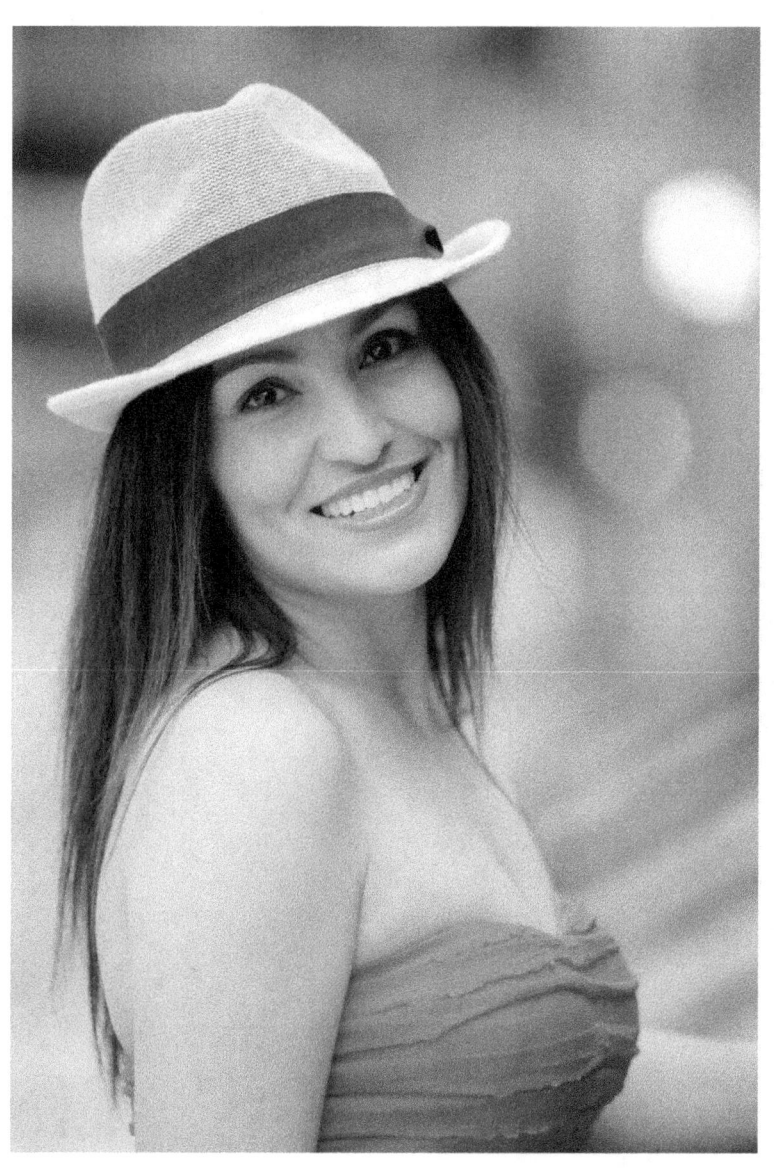

In a full body picture, you must take everything else into account that will be visible in the picture, including any shadow from the subject on the background.

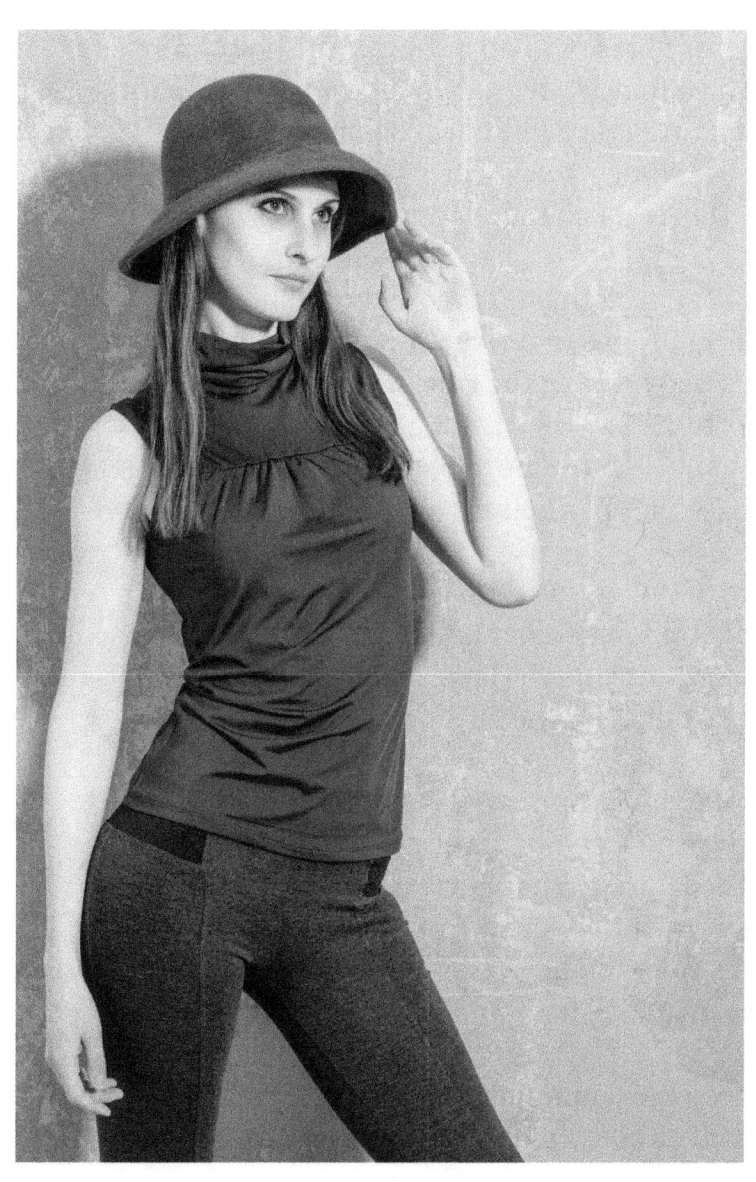

In full body shots, you do not want the body to be strait. Have the subject turn the parts of their body to look natural. Straight lines look posed and unnatural. Notice how all parts of her body are curved, this is much more appealing.

In the chest up shot, and the full body shot, do not have straight lines or straight on facing of the subject's body. Using the rule of thirds will help most portraits as well. If you have open space like the shot above, have the subject looking into the open space, it looks better.

The rule of thirds, in a nutshell, is taking the full frame of your viewfinder and dividing it into nine squares. Many cameras have a grid that you can turn on to help you with using the rule of thirds.

The grid divides your frame into 9 sections, like you would draw when you played tic tac toe as a kid. The rule of thirds says. You want to put the main subject of the photo on one of the four sections in the grid where the lines cross. Where do you want the viewer to look first when they look at the shot?

This photo is a combination of filling the frame, with a longer body photo. To make a shot like this, you must have a solid background that does not affect the shot at all.

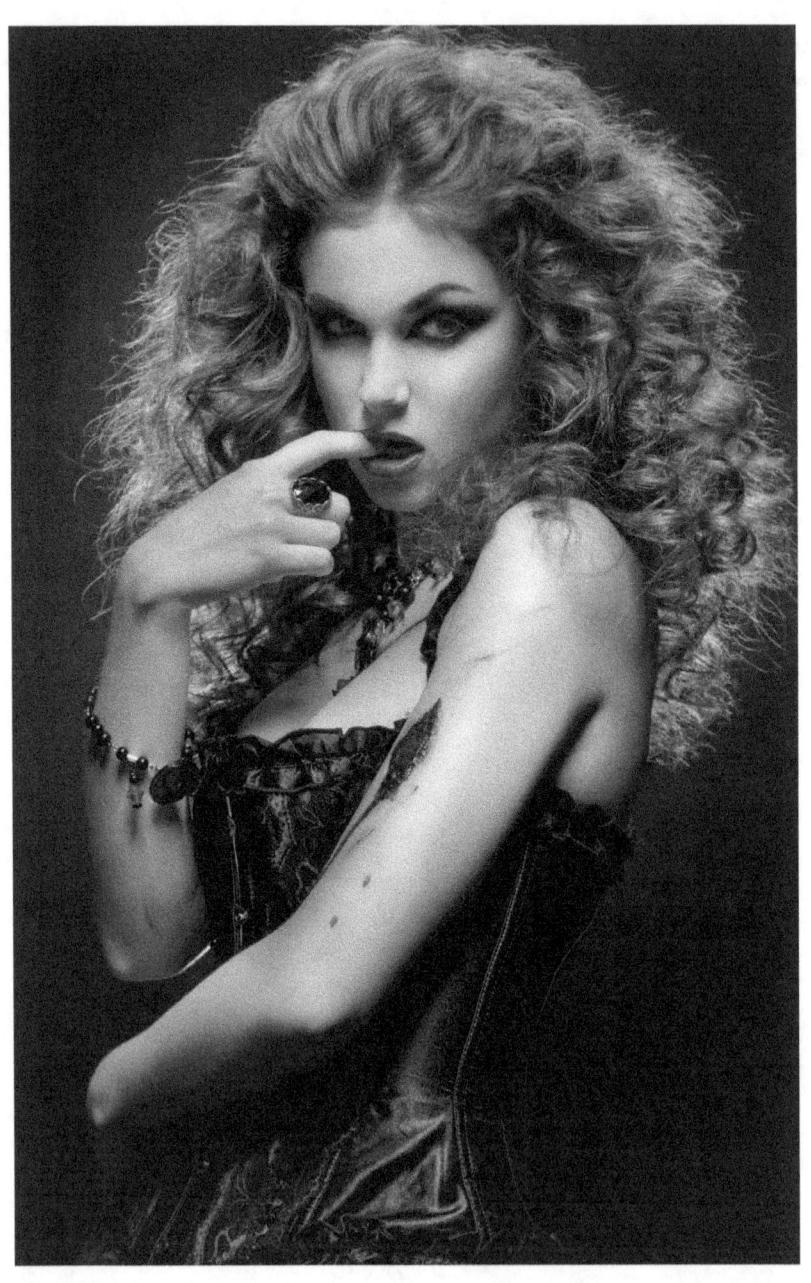

This shot shows how to use the rule of thirds to position the subject in front of a background that does not detract from the main point of the photo that is to get a great face picture. You could crop this shot and it would still be a good shot. It depends on what you are looking for.

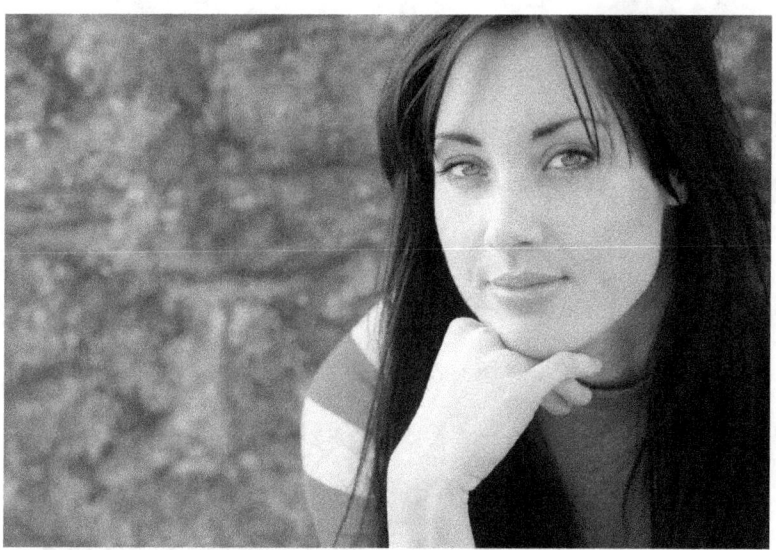

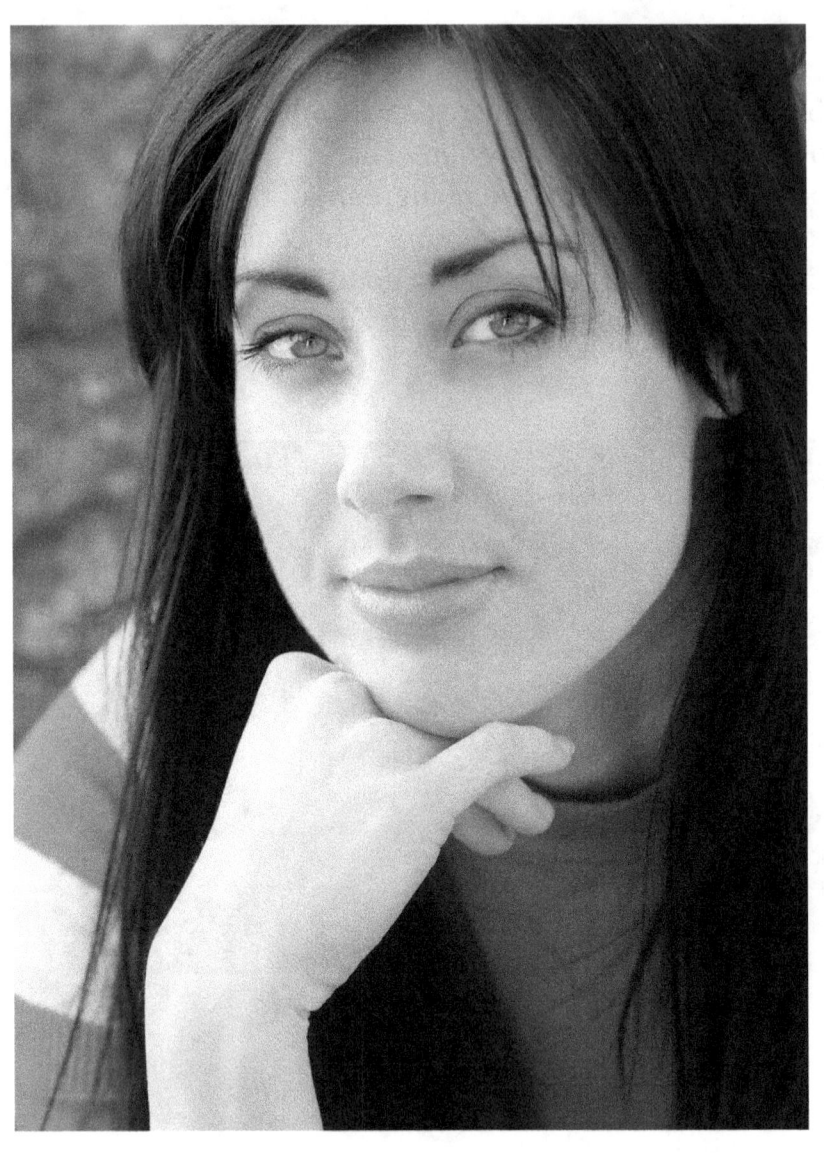

The next shot is a great fill the frame shot. The subject of the picture is obviously a beautiful young woman for sure, but there is no chance that you can view this shot without being drawn immediately to her gorgeous eyes.

The last photo in this section shows how to get a full body shot while using the background to add interest to the scene, without taking away from it. To get a full body shot, you are going to have to have other things in the frame. If you do it right, it works well.

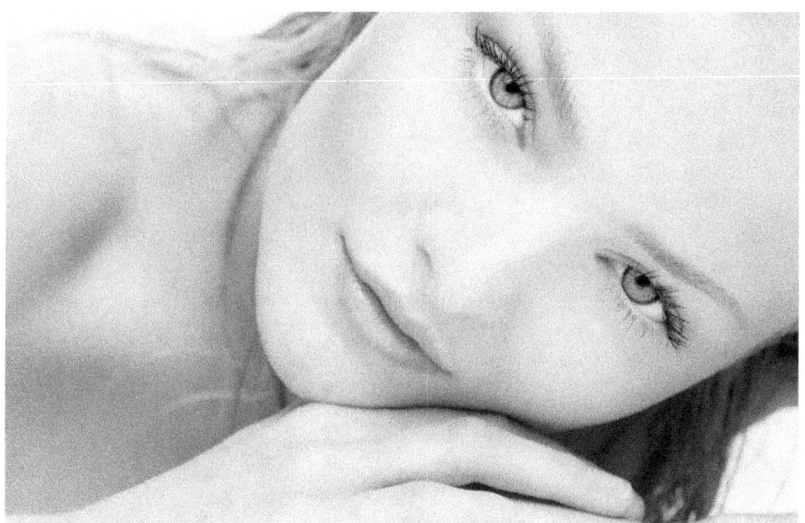

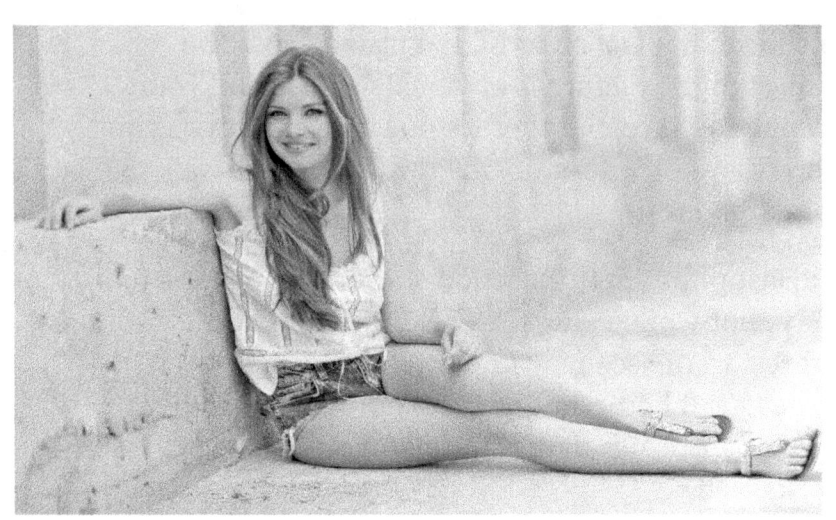

Lighting

Studio Lighting

Studio lighting is where you have the subject illuminated by a flash gets triggered by the camera. You use umbrellas or soft boxes to soften the light. These lights are expensive and not something the average person is going to get.

You can get similar results by using constant lights in a studio like setting. If you get creative, you can get fantastic shots this way by bouncing the light off the ceiling or walls to soften it. Even have a reflector or a diffuser in front of it to change the lighting.

If you want to go to the point of using studio flash, there are many great books and videos that will help you with that. The basic principles of lighting photography are the same. The difference is the set up and how you get the various effects of the light on the subject.

Candlelight

This is a method that is fun to do and can give you some great photos that people will love. Candlelight portraits are fun. You can make some awesome shots with candlelight. It gives the photo a warm and peaceful look.

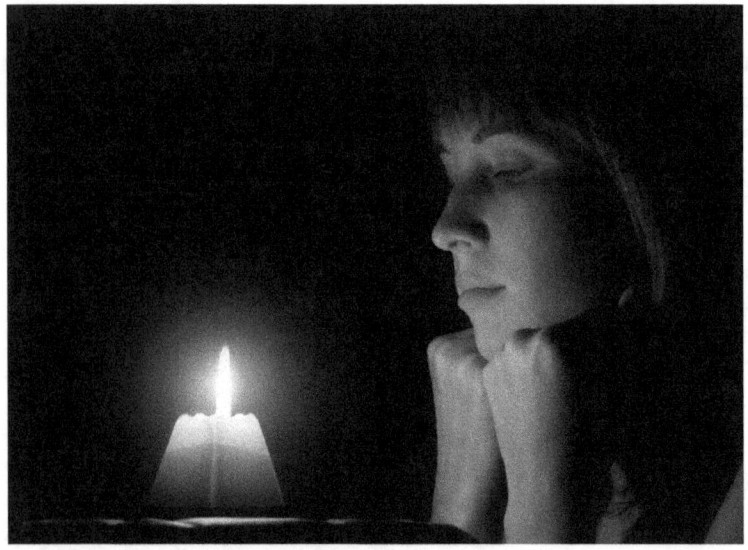

Use a tripod. This is one type of portrait that you will need a tripod if you want to get sharp focus on your shots. There are several types of tripods that will work well for this. I have a tripod that is 12 inches tall and has a clamp that fits my iPhone case; it lets me take great low light shots with my phone.

I also have a Bluetooth remote so I can take the shot from up to 30 feet away. You can shoot it without touching and disturbing the camera. Here are the links to the products on Amazon if you want to try them out.

The cost is about $50 for all three pieces. From what I have found, these are the best tools to get great low light shots with your phone camera. You can hook the camera mount up to any tripod as well. It does not have to be that one, and the Bluetooth remote is awesome.

Camera mount

Bluetooth remote

Tripod

If you are using an SLR, you want to use a bigger solid tripod. One that will keep your camera from moving at all when you are shooting. Set up is key for good candle portraits. Take your time and get it right.

The best setup for candlelight portraits is to use 2 or 3 candles in the scene you want to capture. You will get more even spread-out light that will make for a better shot. Use a single candle if you are going for a portrait that has a harsher side lighting look.

Do not use flash. You do not want to use flash and ruin the candlelight effect.

Use a reflector to fill in any dark shadows on the subject's face. A reflector is useful in better light on the opposite side of the subject's face.

Use a fast lens. If you have a 50mm f1.8 or f1.4, use it for these shots. If you do not have one, you should get one. A 50mm prime lens with f1/8 is the best value you can get in a lens. They are very inexpensive for what you get and are great for many shooting situations.

Shoot in raw mode. Play with the white balance. The auto white balance on your camera may try to compensate for the warm light that you are trying to get. So, try a few settings, or fix it in post processing by shooting in raw mode.

Set the shutter speed slow, but not too slow. If you are shooting a person, you want to keep the shutter speed 1/30 at the slowest, unless they can sit very still. Any slower and you could get blur from any slight movement.

One easy trick that can help the picture is to set up the shot with a table in front. You can shoot above the table, so it is not in the photo. However, if you put a white tablecloth on the table, it will help you get better exposure for the photo. The tablecloth will be your reflector.

The photo below shows what you can do with a single source to get a harsh light look. There are several candles on the left side. However, they are close enough, so the light is all from the same point in the shot and harsh.

If she were looking at the candles, you would see a full front of face shot, and it would completely change the whole look. Play with different shots for the look you want, there are many possibilities with this simple set up.

You can also place a white reflector out of the shot on the right side and it will light that side of her face. It just depends on the look you want.

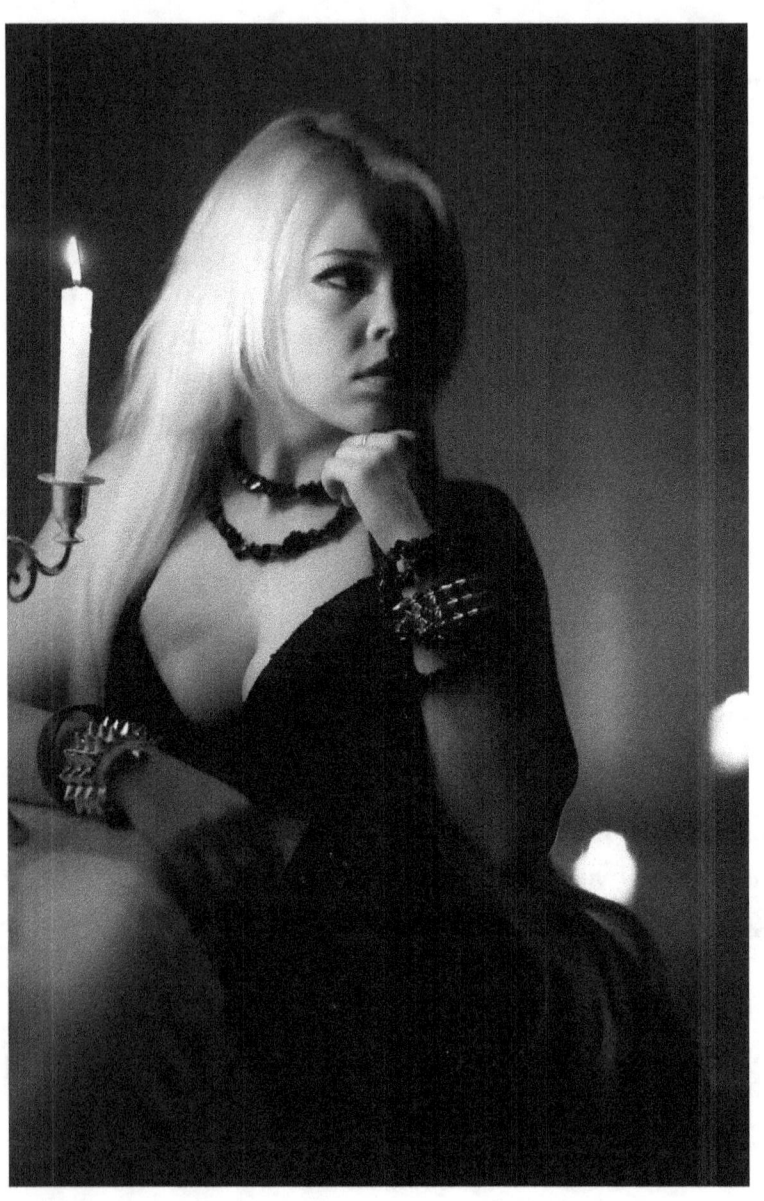

Candlelight photography can be tricky to make work the way you want. One of the great advantages of digital cameras is that you can see right away if you need to alter settings to get the shot you want. You can get some cool photos and it is worth giving it a try.

Window Light Portraits

This is probably my favorite type of indoor portrait. You can get a wide range of effects from window light shots, from very harsh, to soft and sexy.

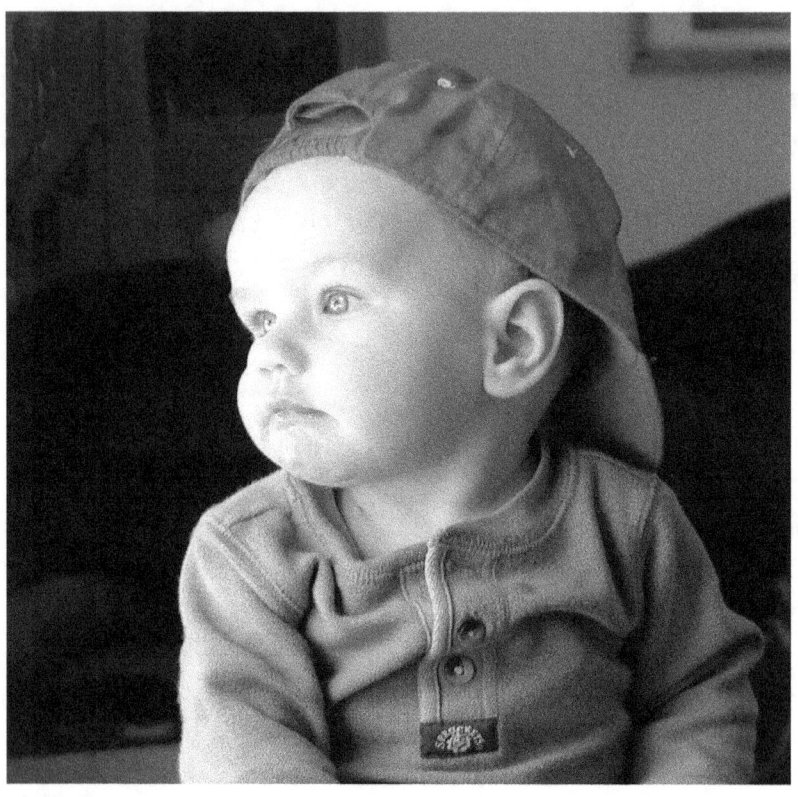

This portrait is one of my favorite window light
shots I have ever taken. This is my grandson
looking out the front window of our house. This was
mid-day with a north-facing window. I used a white
reflector lying on the table between him and the
window. The pose lasted for only a few seconds.
Being ready to snap the shutter when it comes is
critical when you are making pictures of kids. I had
a button in my hand to fire the camera on the

tripod. I moved the reflector and said to him look and pointed out the window and snapped it when he turned his head. Such a great memory. He is an adult now, but I still love the shot.

When shooting window light portraits, it is frequently better to do it like this. Often it adds to the photo if you show the window in the picture, it all depends on your plan and what you see in the shot.

There are even some cool shots you can take from outside the window. Use the widow as a prop in a way and get fantastic lighting like the one below. You can use the window as a soft-focus filter to get the desired look.

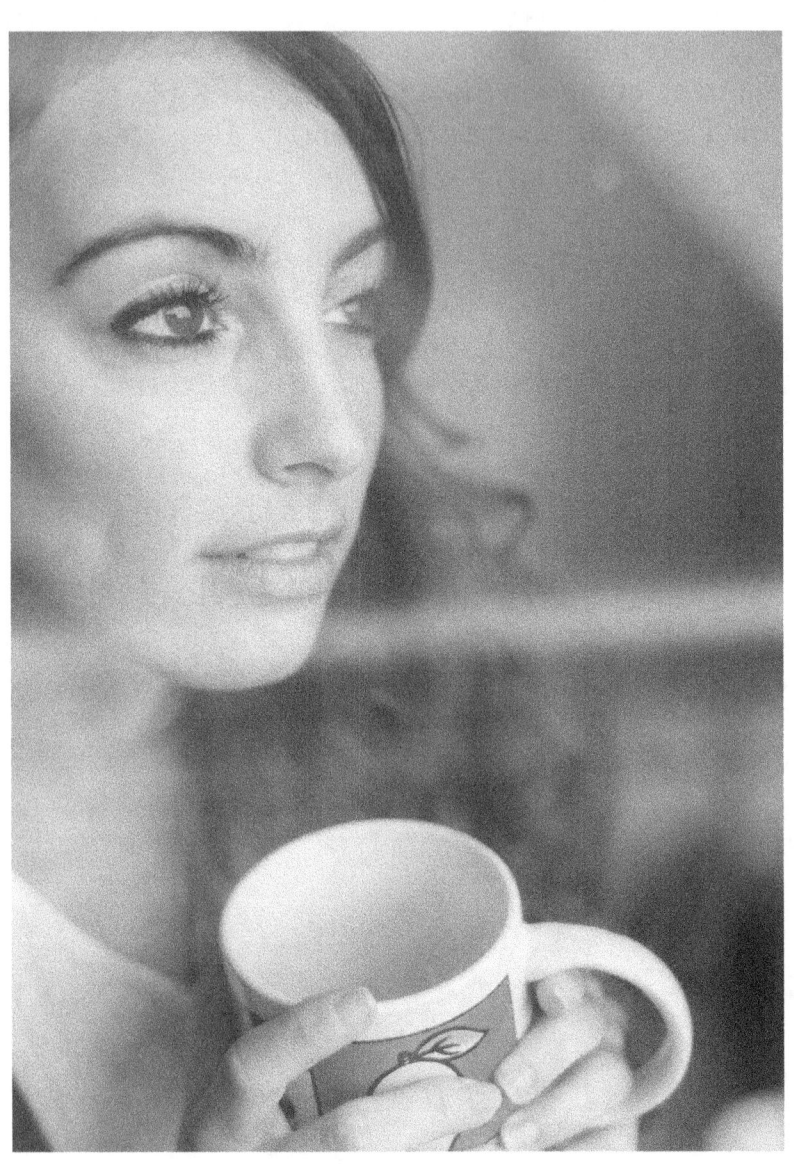

Be careful of the glare from the glass in the photo. Change your angle to get rid of glare, especially if you take it from the outside.

When doing any window light portraits? A North-facing window will almost always work best. If you do not have a North facing, use an East facing in the afternoon or a West facing in the morning. You want to have the sunlight not coming directly in the window.

Window light portraits are fun and can give you years of great memories to cherish.

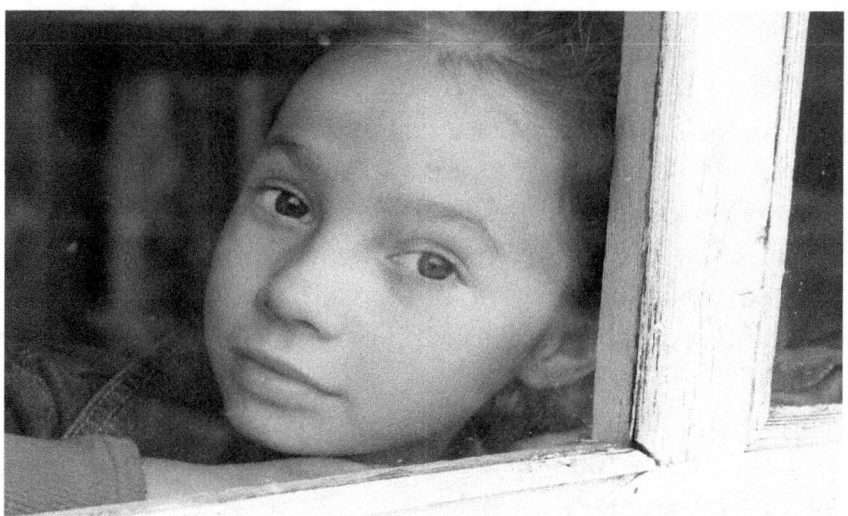

Natural Lighting

I like to do most of my portrait shots with as much natural lighting as I can. Portraits made with sun lighting are much warmer and are more natural. They are closer to the way you see people, and that makes the portraits better because it is more candid.

Using natural light will make you become a better photographer. It makes you focus with the light. Where it is coming from, where it is shining, the intensity, etc. It then makes you do what you need to do to compensate or use the light that is there.

Another huge benefit of natural lighting is that you do not have to buy artificial and stands. You do not have to buy backgrounds and all the other expenses that go into regular studio type lighting. You also do not have to reposition the lights between shots, and you do not have to worry about extension cords, electricity, and batteries.

The position and direction of the light are set for you by nature. You move the subject and where you shoot from to make it work.

Using shade and reflectors you can control the sun to get the lighting and the affects you want. There are sometimes when you want to use the harsh light for effect. Those times are early and late in the day because of the warmer light.

Get out of the harsh direct sunlight into a shady spot or use a reflector of some kind. Get the light back into the subjects face for a pleasant photo.

Another technique that works well in many shots is to have your subject in the shade. And have her hair hit by the sun. It has the effect of a hair light that is used most of the time in studio photography. Use a reflector on the left side to get light onto her face and you are set.

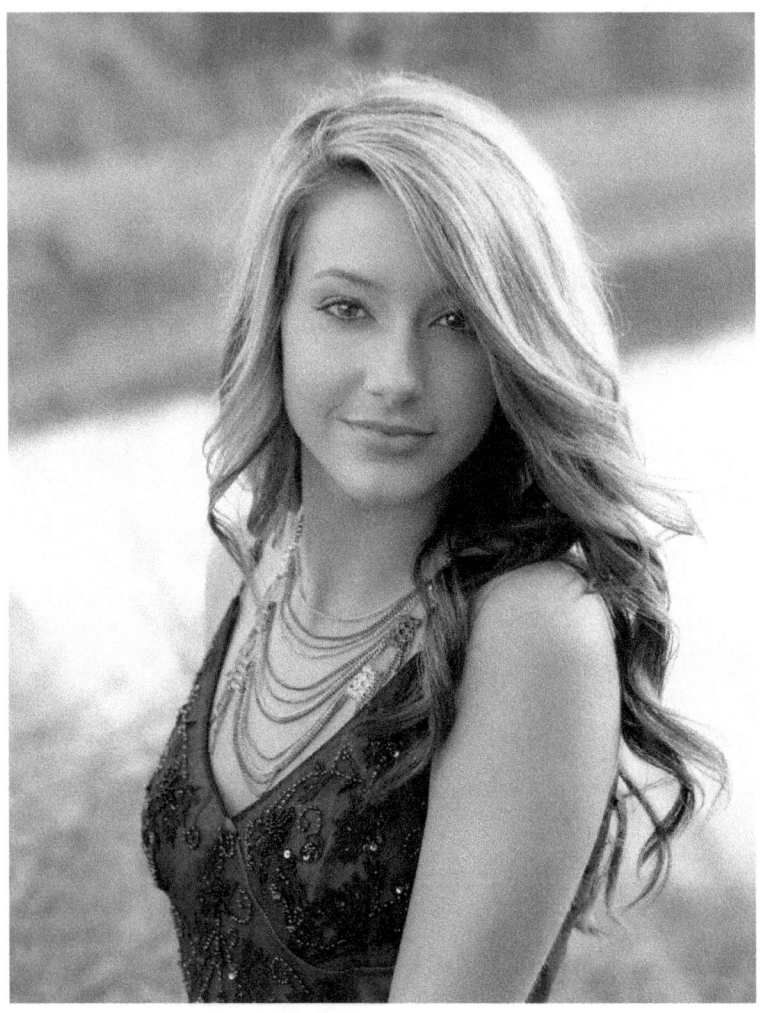

Here is how to check for other cool ideas.
Because of the internet, there are unlimited photos to look at to get ideas. Search Google for a type of shot. Then click on images and get thousands of

examples of how you can set up shots. Get used to looking at other good shots, use the techniques you see to create your own, it will make you a better photographer.

High Key Portraits

High key portraits are portraits that are lighter than what you would shoot most of the time. They are awesome with the right subject and perfect lighting. They can make stunning portraits. High key photos are not easy to set up and do, but if you get it right, they are well worth the effort for the results.

Here is a great example of a stunning high key portrait. What is the first thing you see when you look at this photo?

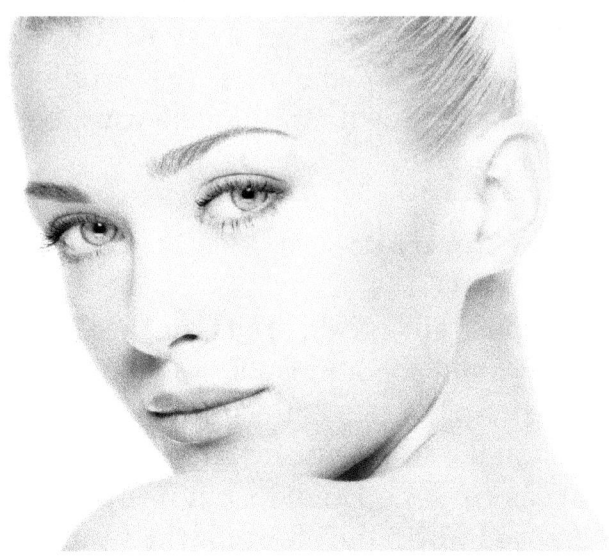

Her beautiful blue eyes must be the first thing you
see. The white background and the very bright skin
force your eyes to go right to her eyes. The one
thing that is contrasting in the shot, those blue eyes.

This photo would be a good shot, even if not high
key. But making the photo high key adds much
more interest and a wow effect and makes it a great
photo.

Use a white background and strong lighting for
good high key photos. Most high key photos will
need studio lights to do right. Without studio flash,
you cannot get enough light on the subject or
background without having highlights blown out in

the rest of the shot. You can still make it work; you need to have the background far enough away from the subject so you can get it light enough.

HIGH KEY PORTRAIT

High key images look great with the right shot. Some of them are stunning even though there is not much detail in the shot. You need a good portrait with a good face shot that is sharp and focused on the eyes. A light background also helps. Most are done in black and white for best effect.

- Open the image you want to use.
- Copy the image.
- Crop to have just the parts you want in the shot.
- Desaturate the image.
- Duplicate layer and blend using screen.
- Open the curves tool and set it close to this.

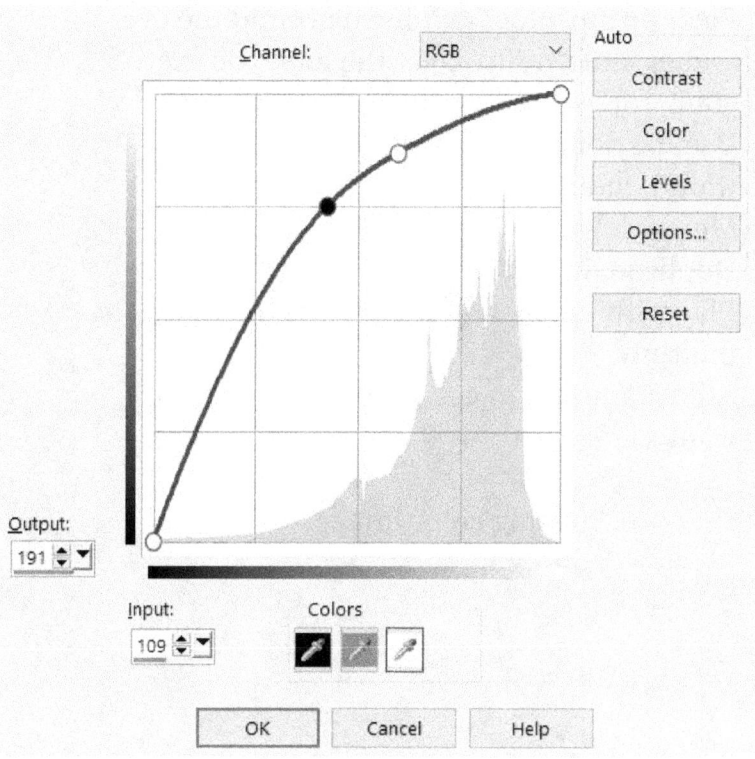

- Flatten layers and merge down.
- Duplicate the adjusted layer.
- Apply Gaussian blur to the top layer, a radius of 18 to 20 pixels.
- Then go to the top layer and in the blend, mode select overlay.
- Adjust the opacity down a bit.

- Pick the burn tool and burn around the eyes and mouth until you get the look you are going for.
- Use the dodge tool to lighten any areas you want lighter.
- Merge down and flatten.
- Duplicate layer again.
- Play with the blend mode. I like to darken, or multiply.
- Adjust amount to get the perfect look you want.

Starting color image

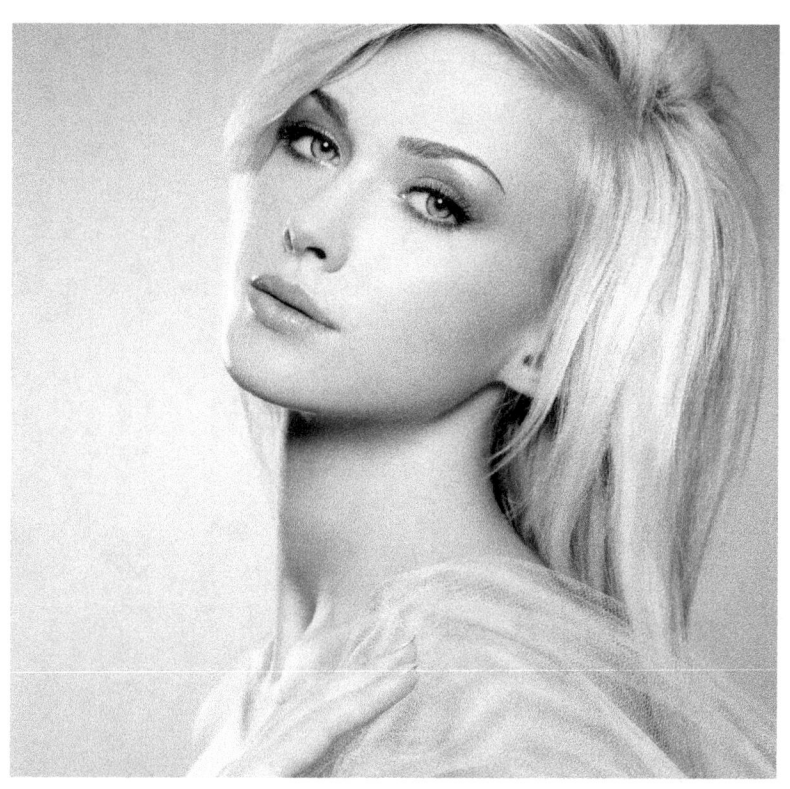

High Key image

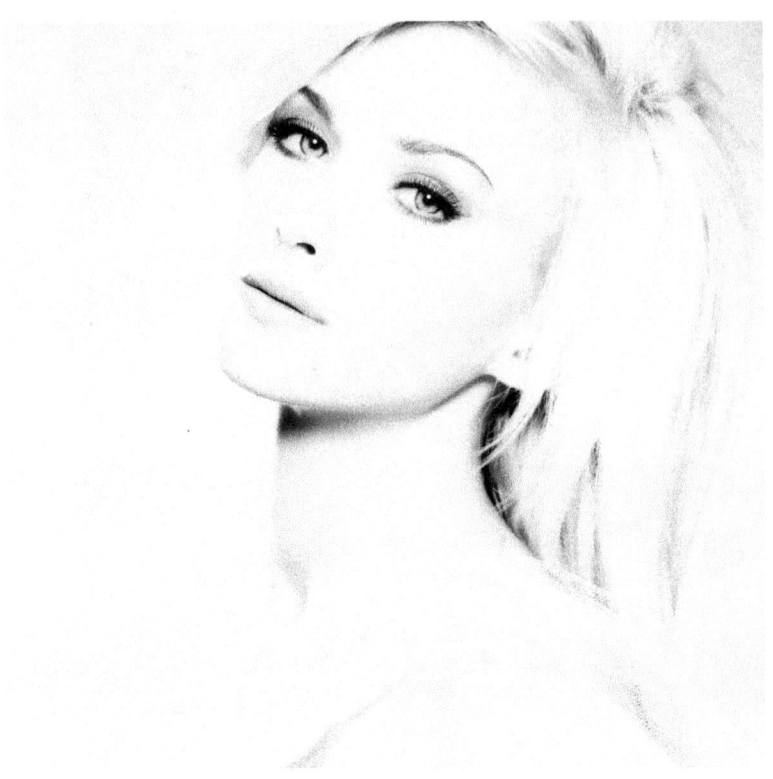

As you can see, she is stunning either way, but the high key gives a different look. Different mood and different impression.

Here is another example done with the instructions above.

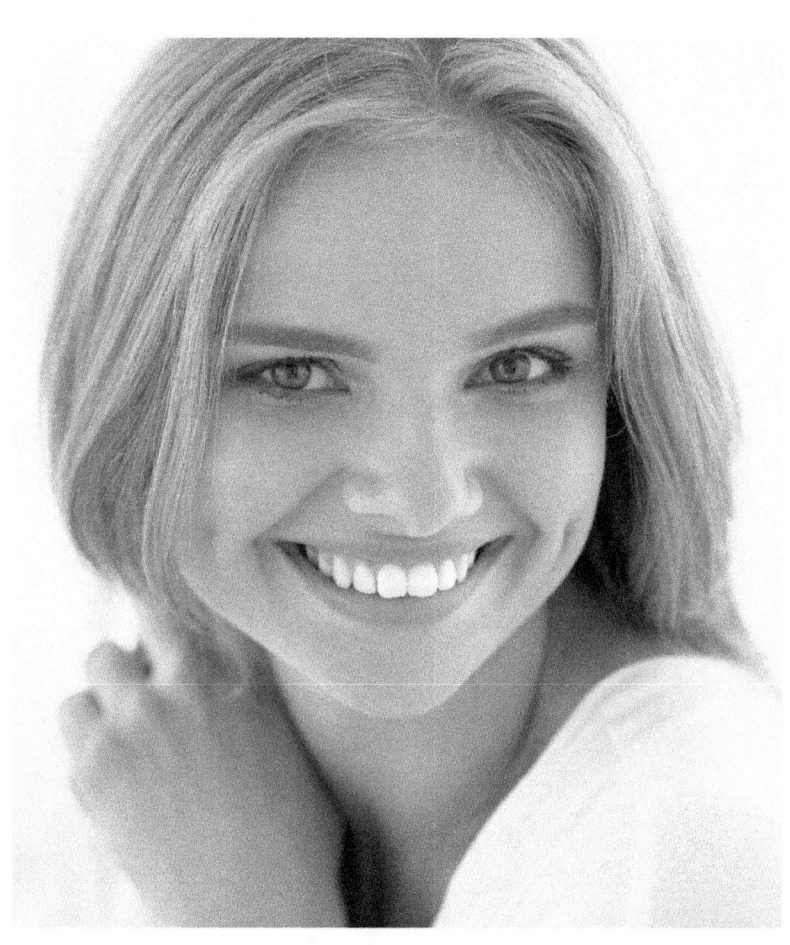

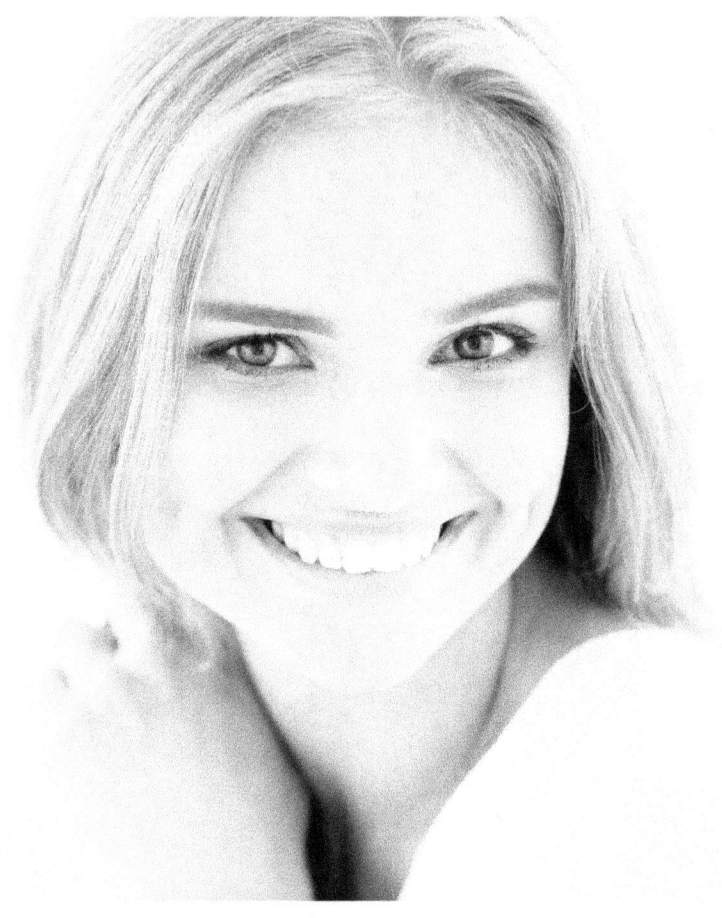

As you can see there is nothing wrong with the color versions of these shots. The high key gives a quite different mood and different look for the right application.

SILHOUETTE PORTRAITS

Silhouettes are easy to shoot, but you can do a lot to make them great shots.

The main key to great silhouettes is a bright light source. The best source for a great silhouette is the sun. The key to exposing for great silhouettes is to expose for the background. Meter the light source and then focus on the subject. You want to have the subject in focus for the best picture.

If you can expose the shot right next to the subject and lock it. Then move the focus on to the subject, you can get the shot you want.

This shot I took with my iPhone with a little tweaking after the shot in post processing. The cool thing about this shot is that this shot is the perfect relaxing shot of my wife. When she is at the lake, this is what she does. She loves to fish from the dock, so it is the perfect way to picture her.

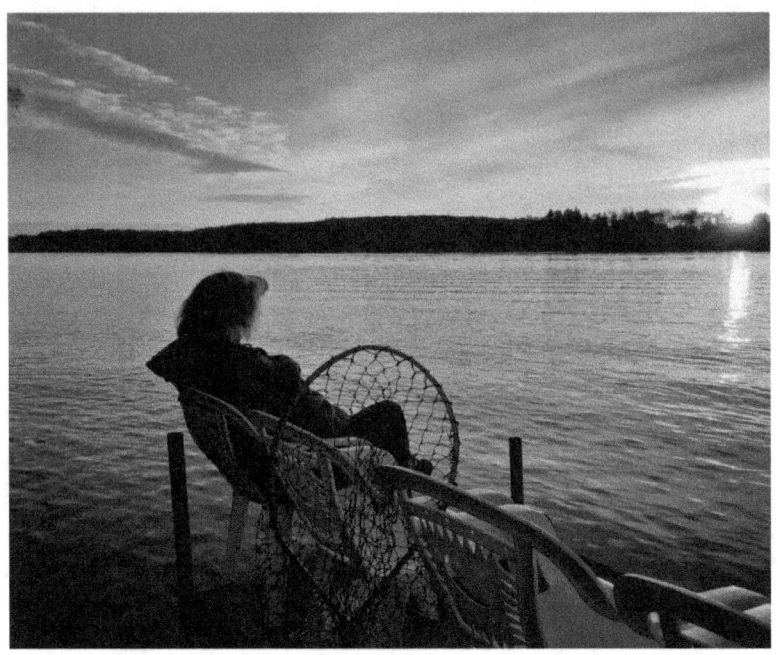

Therefore, we make pictures, to remember the best things we experience. The better the photos are, the better the memories of those moments are.

Here is a shot I took of my son-in-law at the lake. This is another silhouette shot taken with my iPhone. You can get great shots with the new cameras that are on our phones.

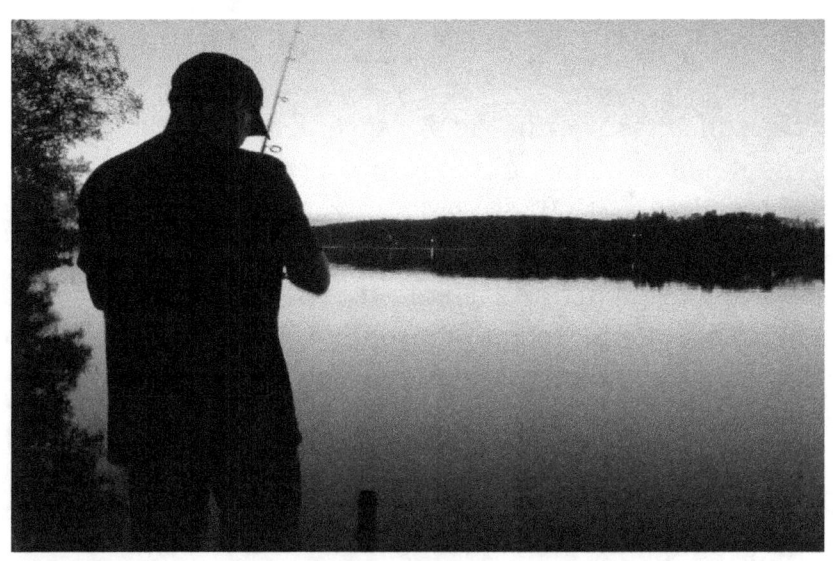

Silhouettes do not have to be taken at sunset; you can take them any time of day. Expose the shot for the sun, or the bright light source. The bright light will make a silhouette of the objects in front of the light source.

Experiment with silhouettes and you will see how much fun they are to shoot. You will learn how you can make some fantastic portraits. These will be excellent lasting memories with silhouettes.

SUNSET PORTRAITS

As the sun gets lower in the sky several things about the light change. The light gets much warmer; it has a golden glow to it. It also creates several lighting issues. The low angle warm light can be harder to use for lighting portraits. Harsh side lighting is sometimes difficult to get the best lighting on the subject's face, and enough light on the rest of the subject.

Use a diffuser to cut the harshness of the setting sunlight. Have someone hold the diffuser to block the sun from the subject's face while being out of the shot. Or use a reflector on the side away from the sun.

If you want to get the subject with the sunset in the shot. You are going to have to use fill flash, or if you have a big enough reflector. A large white reflector should work well. You can put it between the camera and the subject and reflect the light back into the face of the subject.

This will work, but you must have a big reflector, or sand and some hand-held reflectors. The reflector must be far enough back so you can make the photo and keep the reflector out of the shot.

You will have to experiment with how to use the fill flash. The problem is you will not have much time; the good light is gone fast early and late in the day. You will have only about 15 to 20 minutes at most to get the shot with the best sunset or sunrise.

Set the fill flash to as little as you can and get the lighting on the subject's face that you want. If it is too strong, it looks overdone. The key is to make it look as natural as you can.

You want to have it look like there is no flash. Most people in taking a quick look will not notice the flash. That is what you want. If a photographer looks at the shot for a minute. They will see that there could not be enough light coming from that direction without the use of flash. However, if it looks natural, it is good.

This shot is what is a perfect amount of fill flash. The faces look natural, even though the main light source, the sun, could not have lit their faces up like that. You could also do this with the right reflector between the camera and the girls.

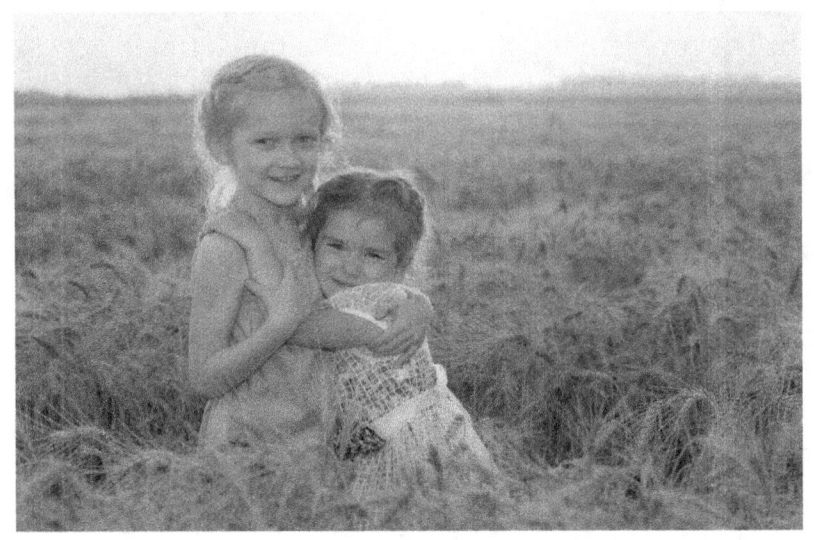

What a great picture, and a great memory.

General Portrait Tips for all Portraits

You do not take a photograph you make it.

Ansel Adams

Photos are a personal thing, but they can stir emotion even in a stranger, when looking at the photo. Make sure that your portraits are personal to either the subject or to you. If you are not making photos for money as a pro, you are likely taking them for yourself or someone special to you.

Make sure that the surroundings in the picture adds more to the memory. Like a special place, you spend time with the subject, or something special that you do there together. The greater the emotion stirred the longer you will enjoy the photo.

When selecting a location for your portrait, make it a place that is meaningful for the subject or to you. The shot can also capture a memory of an event that was important to you or the subject. Depending on who the picture is for. You want the photo to tell a story. The point of a photo telling a story is you only must stir some emotion among the people looking at the shot for it to be a huge success.

This shot is a fantastic shot that captures a memory of a special day and special time that will be a memory for her family and even for her for years to come. And how cute is that.

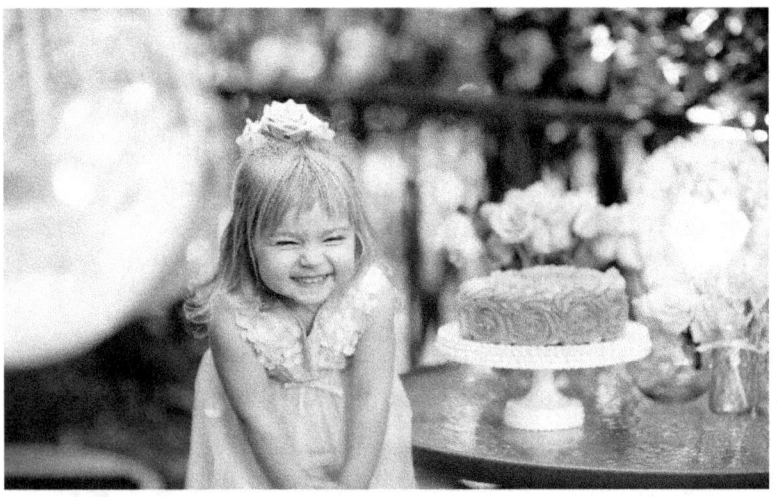

Part of picking the location is determining the background, to determine the best background, you need to decide if you want the background as part of the shot in focus. Or do you want it blurred and have it be more of a way to stop the viewer's eyes from going beyond the subject?

If you want to blur the background, try to pick a background that is a uniform color if possible. It looks better if there is nothing to distract from the subject.

Parks and gardens make for great backgrounds. You can use flowers and trees as part of the portrait. Or you can blur them and still have an interesting background. However, have it out of focus so it does not detract from the subject. Foliage on trees works well out of focus.

When shooting outdoor portraits. Look for leading lines or framing of the subject to draw the viewer's eyes right where you want them to look.

Objects like fences, streams, walls, and railroad tracks. These items all make great leading lines to draw the viewer into the shot.

Framing can be done with anything that draws the viewer's eyes into the shot. Trees work well; standing on a sidewalk is a great leading line. Anything that stops the viewer from looking away from the subject is a good frame. If it is not more interesting than the subject.

Furthermore, when shooting outside, look for areas of open shade, or shade that is from something that you want to use in the shot.

The frame does not have to be at the same depth with the subject. You can make great shots with the frame in the foreground or in the background of the shot.

Here is a framed photo that works very well.

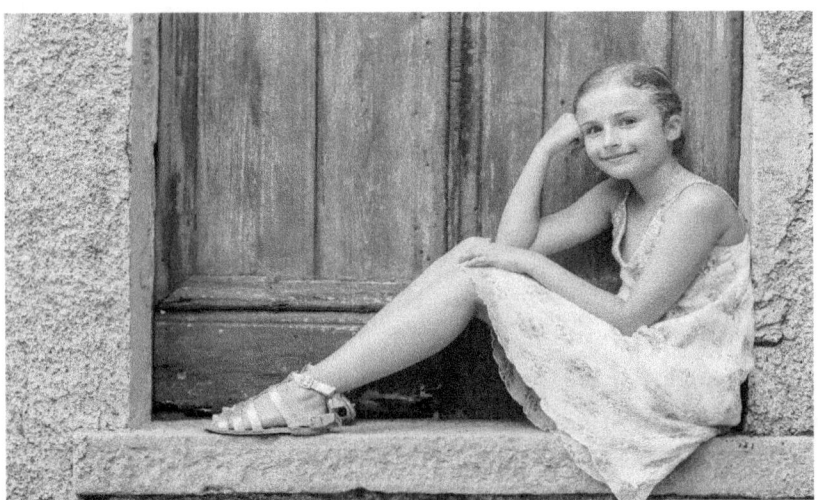

Do not let your camera select the focus points for you. Most DSLRs will let you pick the focus point of the shot. I will have it set for the center of the shot. I can next focus where I want and lock that point, then compose the shot at that point.

Setting the shot up this way, I do not have to worry about changing the composition of the shot. It will always have the focus point on the subject. I took a lot of shots before I learned that setting the focus point was so important. Because the camera would have the focus of the shot not where I wanted it. It is frustrating when you think you have a great shot, and the focus is not on the main subject. You want the subject sharp in focus.

Always focus on your subject's eyes or at least the face if the eyes are not part of the shot. The face and eyes are where you want the viewer to look for almost all portraits. So, you want to have the crisp focus on the face and eyes.

Even if the photo is not a close up shot, like the one above, still always focus on the face and eyes.

Here is an example of a classic portrait pose, with the subject leaning against a wall. You have a leading line that draws the viewer's eyes straight to the subject. You have the scene framed on one side by the wall, and on the other side by the edge of the photo. This type of pose gets used often because it works so well.

There are a lot of variations to this pose. You can crop it closer to the subject and make it a great close up, that changes the entire look and mood of the picture.

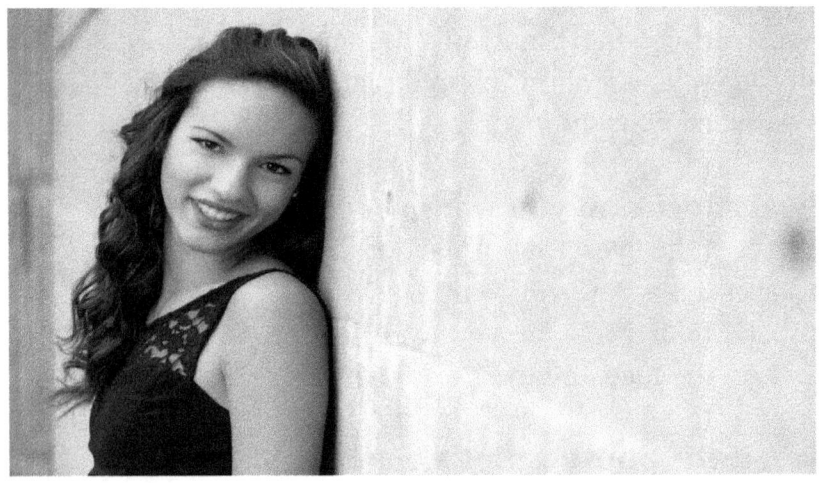

If it is cropped, you still have the leading line. At the same time, you have the shot framed. You also have the background that does not draw away from the subject. And you have a great shot any photographer would be happy with. It depends on what you are going for with the photo.

This is another reason why shooting your portraits in raw mode will allow you to do more with your shots. The shot above when cropped to the next shot, takes a lot of resolution and detail from the shot.

When you crop your photo, you will still have enough in the cropped shot to make good prints if you want.

Use a polarizer if the subject is wearing glasses, it will cut the glare almost completely.

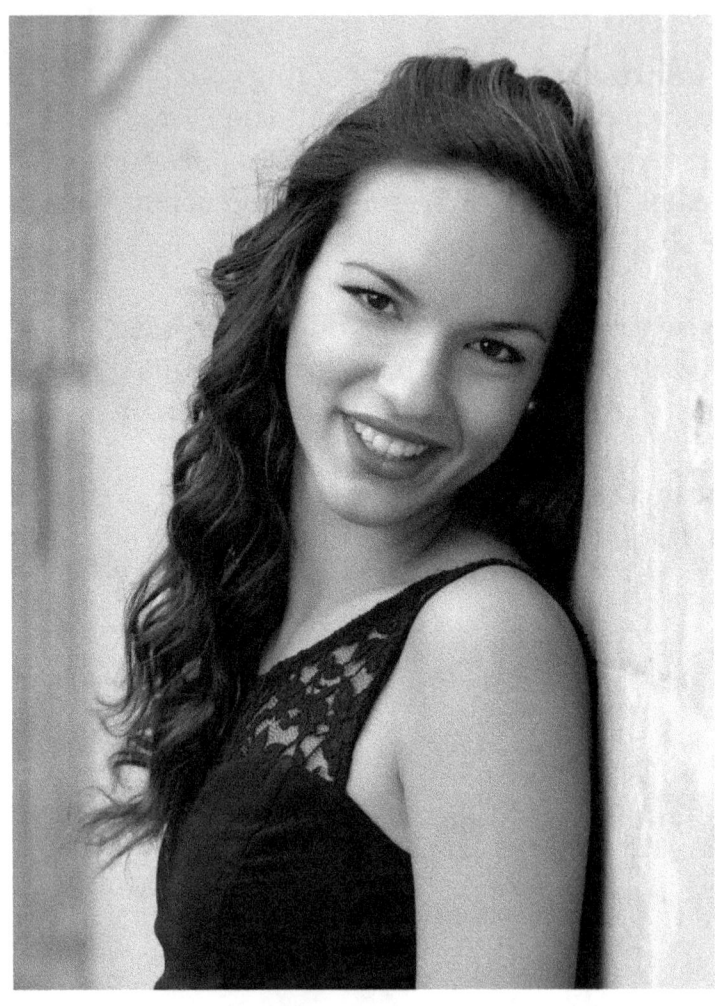

Do not shoot portraits with a lens shorter than 50mm. There are a few cases when you can break this rule and get some interesting shots. However, they are not generally flattering shots and are more for being different. Remember with a digital camera, your focal length is about 1 ½ times longer than what the focal length is of the lens. Unless you have a full-frame camera.

You should carry a compass in your camera case for shooting on cloudy days. You can also use the compass on your cell phone. Even when it is cloudy, the sunlight is still coming from a certain direction. The light may not be direct, but it is still directional. On cloudy days, put the sunlight at your back, and you are ready to go.

Spend some time before you start shooting to get to know your subject. Relate to them and make them feel comfortable. This will make your portrait shots better in any type of portraiture. Be it kids, men and women, groups, or couples. Make them feel relaxed and everything will work much better.

Get closer to the subject. Sometimes you need to use a longer lens to get nearer. If possible, move tighter to the subject. Sometimes using a longer telephoto lens and zooming in can give you the best shots.

Be prepared to make the shot. Especially when you are taking candid shots, constantly be prepared to take the shot. You will miss some great shots if you are not always alert.

Pay attention to the rule of thirds when composing your shots. Look through the viewfinder and compose the shot. Look at the background, foreground, and all the elements that will be part of the shot. Position the subject in the correct place in the shot. You can change this in post processing, but it is always better to try to get the best shot when you take it. Never think you can fix it later when you are taking a shot. Try to get it right when you take it. The less post processing you must do, the better.

Try some unexpected things that break the photography rules. Sometimes you get some great shots breaking the rules. Do not miss taking the shots that follow the rules.

Turn the camera and shoot in portrait mode. Other than professional photographers, over 90% of all photographers shoot in landscape mode all the time. Using phone cameras more people shoot in portrait mode because that is the way the camera is normally held. Shoot in portrait mode to get the best portraits. That way, you do not have to crop the photo to make a good portrait. Cropping is ok, but you get less detail in the shot when you crop it. If you crop a lot, the detail loss will be significant.

Shooting with your lens at eye level of the subject is the most common and generally the best way to shoot portraits. To get some interesting variations shoot below the eye line or from up high on some shots. Sometimes shooting from a significantly low angle also works well. Do the most common and likely shots for portraits. Do not forget to try unusual shots as well. You have nothing to lose and a lot to gain if you get a great shot.

If the subject has a good side, make sure you have them turn so you will flatter their best side. Do all you can to make the subject look their best for portraits. Everyone wants to look good in pictures, and you want the subject, and your goal is for the subject to love the shot.

Shooting into the light can make for some great photos. If you do it outdoors in bright light use a lens hood. This will make it much easier to get the lighting right.

Switch your camera to black-and-white shooting occasionally. You will be able to see how the shot will look in black and white. It is easy to convert any color shot to black and white. But you should look at the shots that way sometimes to give you the right perspective on how it will look. **I have a book on shooting black and white** that covers black and white portraits in detail.

Here is a great shot that tells a story, has great lighting, and good focus. It shows use of the rule of thirds. It gives the subject space in front of the direction she is looking and captures a great shot. The light source is on the right, a large reflector on the left to light her face.

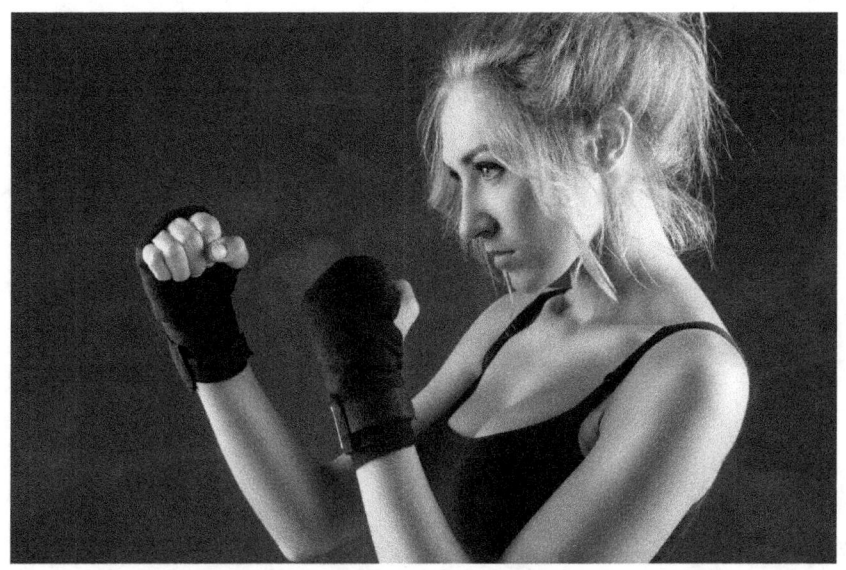

Try some shots with the subject looking away from the camera. When you do this, you can either show what they are looking at, or you can keep it a mystery to the viewer. This shot as you can see is lit from both directions to get the desired effect.

Take some cropped shots. Crop the shot with the composition. Get in close, as close as just the face. Possibly even closer and get only the center of the face to get a unique portrait.

Below is an example of a cropped shot. This shot works well because the subject is a great shot from this composition. This will not work for all people and all types of shots; it takes a special shot for this to work.

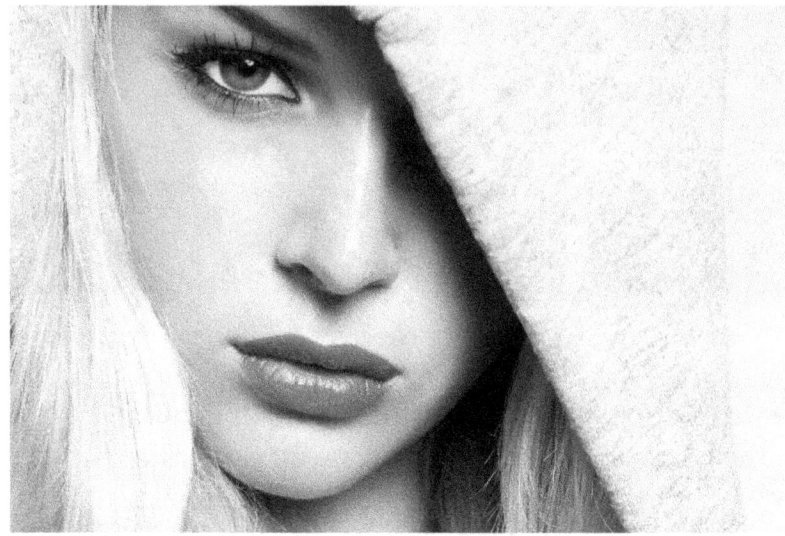

Shoot candid portraits of people doing things. It can be anything that people are doing. Some of my favorites, and some of the best portrait shots I have taken are candid shots of people. Shoot them doing things they like to do. They will relax and not even pay attention to you. Great natural looking shots that do not look posed. Candid shots are not posed and set up, they are natural, and generally capture the person doing something they enjoy doing. Great memories come from candid's because it is something, they like to do and have good memories doing it.

Many subjects I have found when posing smile in a way that looks fake. If you get candid shots of them having fun and enjoying what they are doing, you will get pleasant natural looking smiles.

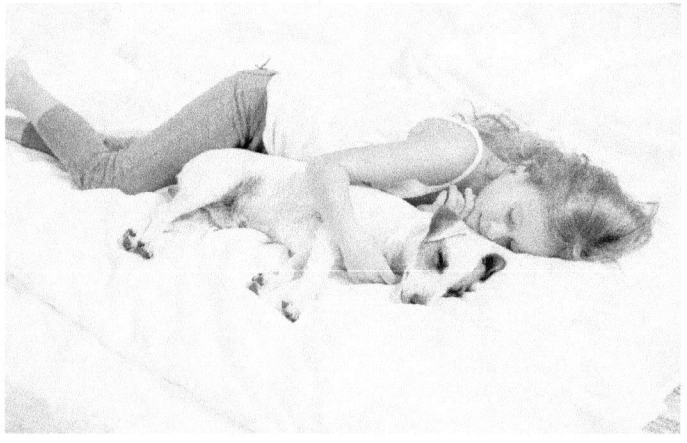

A girl sleeping with her puppy is a great capture that will bring her fond memories.

To get some interesting shots. Turn your camera at unusual angles. Do not shoot in portrait or landscape, turn the camera at 30 degrees or 45 degrees and try something out of the ordinary.

Use props. Props of things that your subject uses when they do things they enjoy. This is one of the best ways to tell a story in your photos.

Special tips for Portraits of Women

Photography is an art of observation, it has little to do with the things you see, and everything to do with the way you see them.

Elliott Erwitt

The most important issue in photographing women is you want to flatter them and make them look beautiful. It also benefits the photographer to flatter them. Everyone wants to look fantastic for the camera.

The key to flattering women and making the shots look excellent is by how you pose them. And if you show their best features. There are a lot of good poses and a lot of excellent looks. This is where you need a swipe file that you can look at. Have shots of your favorite poses. Then you can recreate the poses when you are making pictures, so you can position the subject to look their best.

The basic poses come in full length, ¾ length, head and shoulders, and headshots. Most portraits that you want to capture are shooting the subject in ¾ or head and shoulders. If you are shooting a theme, or you want to show action, the photos are generally full length.

The worse thing you can do in shooting a portrait is to have the subject standing facing the camera with their arms down to the sides. It is not flattering at all. Look at the links below. None of the poses have the subject standing facing the camera with arms at the sides.

Here is a link to a guide on Pinterest that has most of the basic full-length female poses to get the best looks.

Here is a link to a photo posing book that you can get on Amazon, this is the best guide for posing women that I can recommend.

Here is a link to a Digital Photography School post that has 21 good poses to start with when posing women.

Here is a link to part 2 of posing women from Digital Photography School.

Here is the link to part 3 from Digital Photography School for posing women.

Be careful not to shoot with too fast of a lens wide open. Even a slight head turn can put one side of her face and one eye out of focus with such a shallow depth of field. You can get a depth of field down to an inch or so if you are not careful, and that is not enough for portraits.

Shooting subjects with larger waistline. Turn the subject at an angle, never shoot straight on.

Another slimming technique is to shoot from a higher angle.

Another way of slimming is to use a longer lens, so the depth of the shot is not compressed at all.

Always ask the subject if she has features that she wants to show off and ones that she does not care to show.

Turn her body away from you and her head back toward the camera. cover her neck with a collar or a scarf or something so that a deep neck crease does not show.

You may have heard the photography advice, if it bends, bend it. Do not have any straight joints, bend the legs and arms to have no straight joints, it looks much better.

Have her lean toward the camera; the natural tendency is for them to lean away.

If you want to get the best exposure on the subject's face. Use spot metering on the face. If you are shooting a head and shoulders shot, or a head shot, spot metering can work well.

Contrast the clothes with the background. You do not want the subject to blend with the background. You want them to stand out unless you are going for the blend look, or a high key shot.

Diffuse the on-camera flash. I have a nylon diffuser that is cool. It fits around the lens with an elastic piece and goes in front of the flash to soften the light from the flash. If you use a diffuser, you can use your on-camera flash for fill if needed.

Posing women

Generally, a bad pose for women is the subject facing the camera straight on and standing straight up. Turning their body, one way or the other, and not standing straight will almost always make the shot better.

Try to not have any straight lines of the subject. Have them bend their joints and lean to add smooth curved lines.

Lengthening her legs will create better lines. She can wear heels; she can stand on her tip toes, or you can shoot her from the back to lengthen her legs. Legs look longer from the back because the buttocks are part of the legs and make them look longer.

Do not have arms or legs closer to the camera than the body. This will distort the limbs making them look strange.

Socks make legs look shorter. If she is wearing shorts or skirt with socks, removing the socks will lengthen her legs.

Jeans and a tee shirt, or jeans and a sweatshirt will make the subject look younger. Wearing business clothes will make them look older.

Particularly important in posing women.
Make sure you use her hair to advantage and make
her look the best it can be.

Hats are great props that can make her look
more feminine and relaxed.

**If you have concern about the subject's
double chin.** Shoot from a higher position and
make sure that she does not tilt her head forward. A
tilted back head will stretch out the skin on the neck
and keep it from showing a double chin. Shooting at
a higher angle will stretch the skin and pull it
tighter.

Here is a great pose that accentuates everything
about her face, and there are no straight lines. This
shot is very flattering in every way.

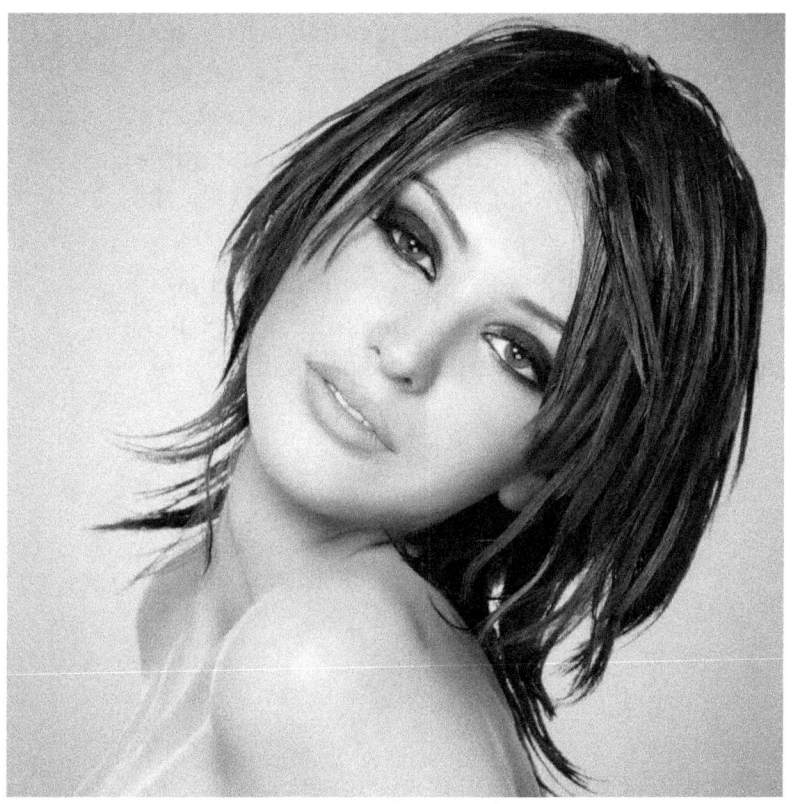

If your subject is seated and her legs are in the picture. It is generally better to have her cross her legs at the ankles instead of at the knees.

If she is seated on the ground, it looks better to have one leg stretched out and the other bent at the knee.

If you have the subject lying on the ground
on her stomach. Have her legs bent at the knees?
Have her ankles crossed. This gives a relaxed and
casual look that is generally flattering to the subject.
And will work for almost any type of photo shoot.

Get down to the subject's level when using this
pose. As you can see, turning the camera on this
shot added a little more interest to the shot.

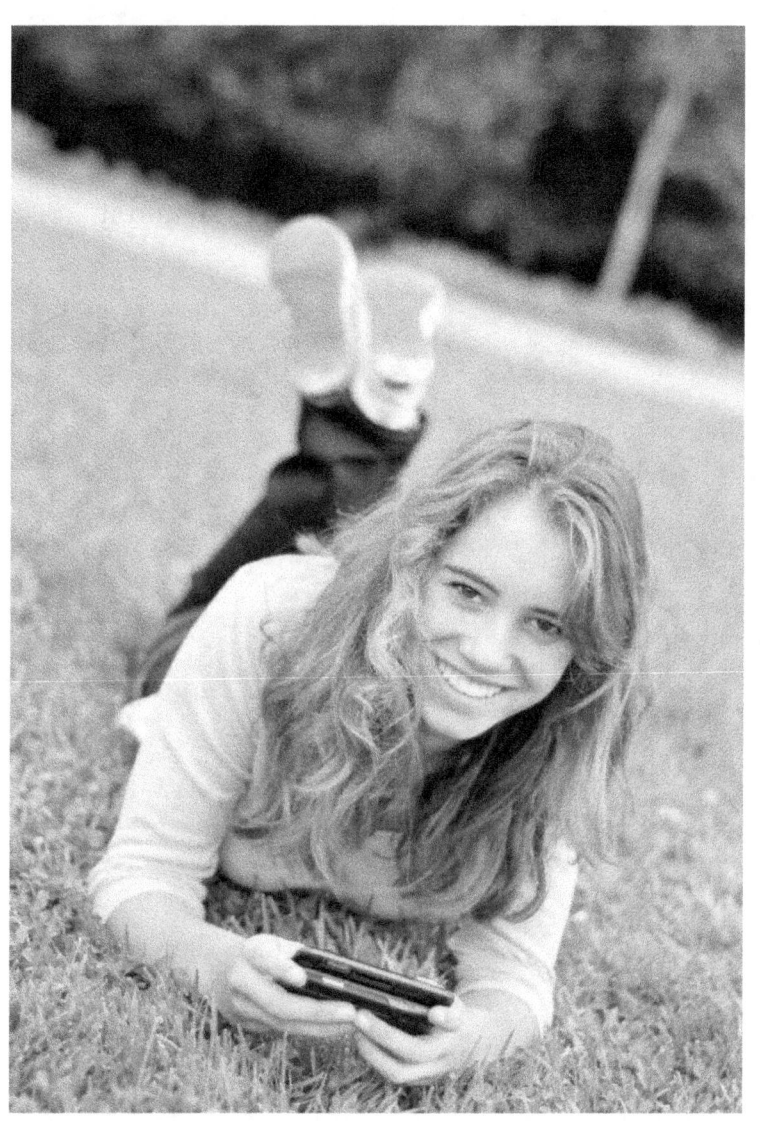

A car is another fantastic prop for shooting in. You can get the subject in the car, have the door open or close, and you can use the shade of being in the car to get a well-lit shot even in direct sun with little problems. In a car the subject is relaxed, and it focuses on the subject.

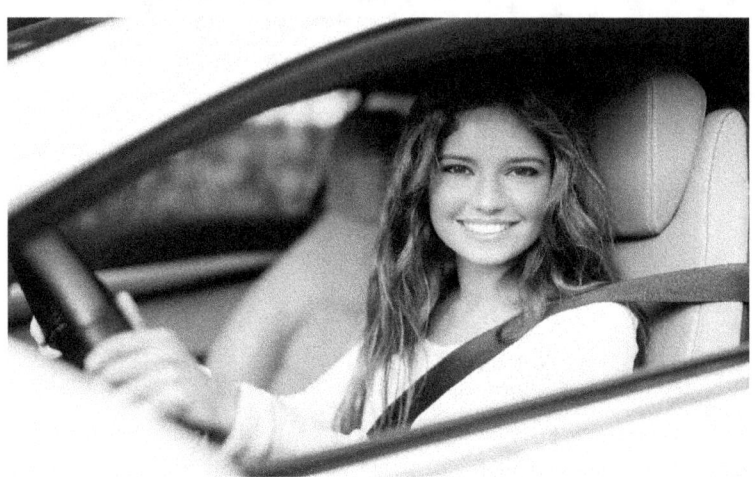

Special Tips for Portraits of Couples

Which of my photographs are my favorites?

The one I am going to take tomorrow.

Imogen Cunningham

Shooting portraits of couples. You want to get to know them and find out what they like, and what they want from the portrait. While you are doing that, get them to relax and to feel comfortable with you.

When you get ready to make the shots, you need to get them to interact with each other. Get them to feel comfortable enough around you that they can be themselves. Then you can capture them relating to each other in a natural way.

Here is one of my favorite couple's shots, it is very natural and shows that they care about each other.

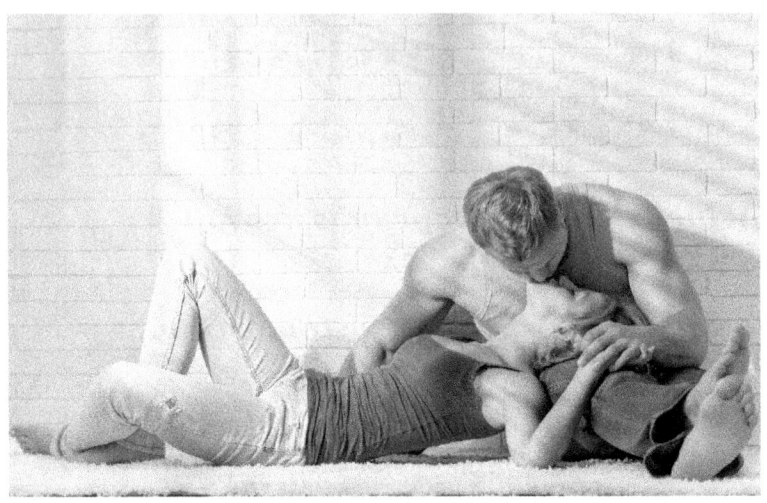

The shot also captures them as you would think they might interact when they are home together.

When shooting couples, hands can be an issue, make sure if they are in the shot, they look relaxed and normal. Make it look like the hands are where they should be. Awkward looking hands can ruin a great shot, make sure they appear natural.

Have the couple look at each other instead of the camera in many of the photos. You will get more intimate and much more interactive shots.

Have a good swipe file of couple's shots. Make sure that you have a few planned ahead of time that you want to recreate.

When you get them interacting with each other, make sure you are ready all the time to get great candid shots.

Try to create a loving mood by shooting the photos at a place that means something special to them. The place they met, their first date. Their first kiss, something that has great passionate memories for them.

Try to make these photos with natural light and use a reflector if you need to. A gold reflector gives a warm tone to the shot. Warmer is better when a romantic shot is important.

Here is a link to a Digital Photography School article on posing couples. A great article with some fantastic poses to get you started.

While you are shooting, make sure all your comments are positive. Make sure you compliment them all through the shoot. This will ensure they stay relaxed and feel free to interact with their partner.

Try some shots with one of them looking at the camera, and the other one looking at their partner. After that switch and have the other one looking at the camera and the partner looking at them.

Do not forget to do some couple's shots in Black and White. Most people like colored photos better. However almost everyone loves a good black-and-white portrait.

Even when the couple is walking away from the camera. You can get a great shot that will give them good memories if it tells a story. Here is a shot I took with the couple walking away from the camera. It was a warm fall scene. And even though you cannot tell who it is. They know it was them, and they remember how they were feeling, and what a fantastic day it was.

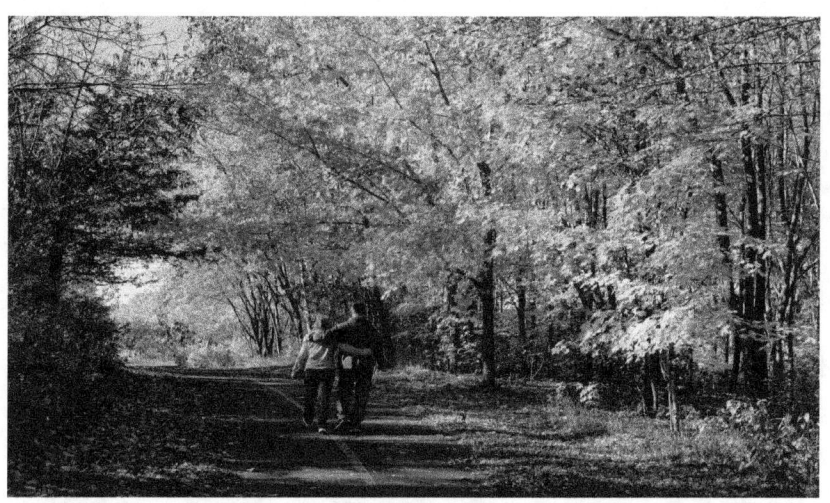

This was a candid shot that they were not even expecting me to take, and it is a favorite because of the memories of that day.

Here is a great couple shot. They are close and intimate and showing them doing something they love to do together. They will have great memories of the perfect time they were having.

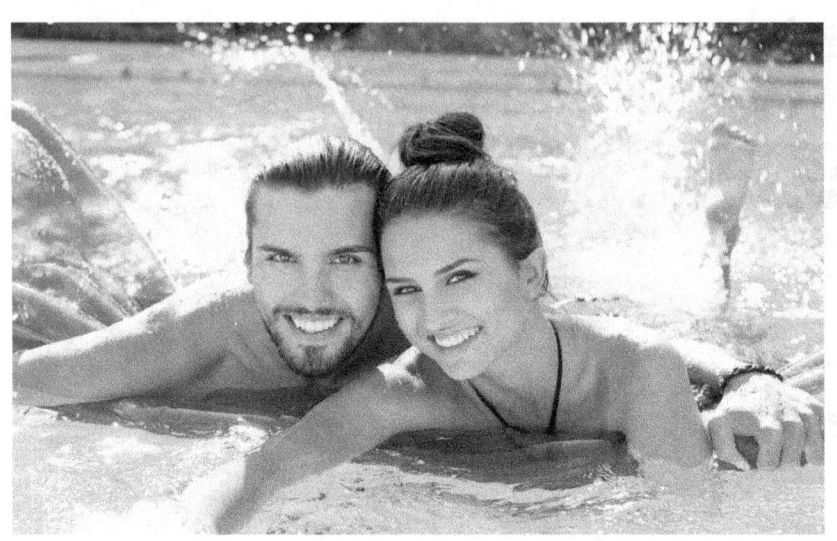

Special Tips for Portraits of Men

Light makes photography. Embrace light. Admire it. Love it.

But above all, know light. Know it for all you are worth, and you will.

Know the key to photography.

George Eastman

If you are shooting a portrait of a man alone, and it is not a head shot, make the shot of him doing something he likes to do. A hobby or a sport or woodworking or painting. Shoot him doing something he is passionate about and enjoys doing.

Here is a link to the Digital Photography School article. It will give you some great poses to start with for positioning men.

Use the poses on the website for more formal portraits. For more relaxed shots, use the tip of getting candids of him doing something he likes to do.

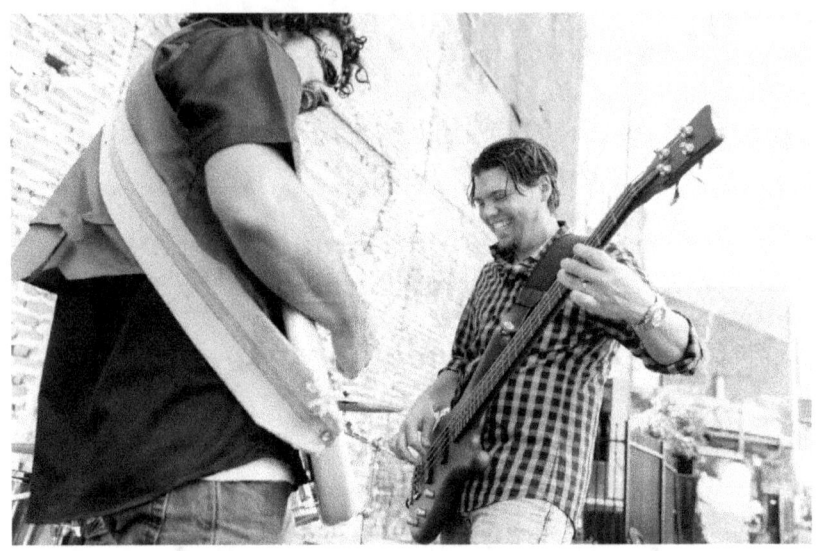

This shot is a great example of what a portrait of him doing something he loves will look like. This is exactly how he wants people to see him, having a great time doing something he loves to do with a good friend.

Here is a good casual shot of a man. It works well for most all other portrait shots for men.

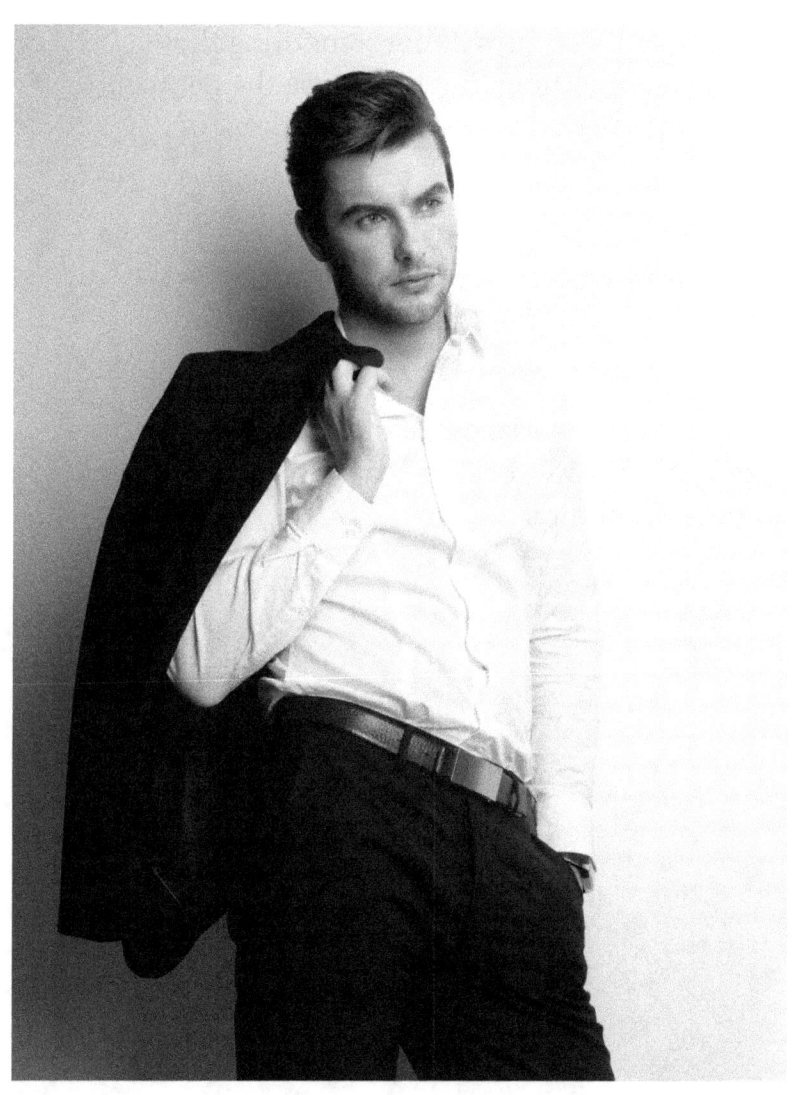

<u>Here is a link to some great inspirational</u> portraits of men. If you look at these photos, you will notice

that they are of these guys doing something they love to do. Or something that will cause the people that see them, say that is exactly how I think of them.

Here is a link to the Digital Photography school page for posing men. 21 poses to get you started. These are good swipe file shot to have for future use.

This guy obviously works out a lot to look like this. Showing him doing a workout is a perfect way to get a great portrait of him.

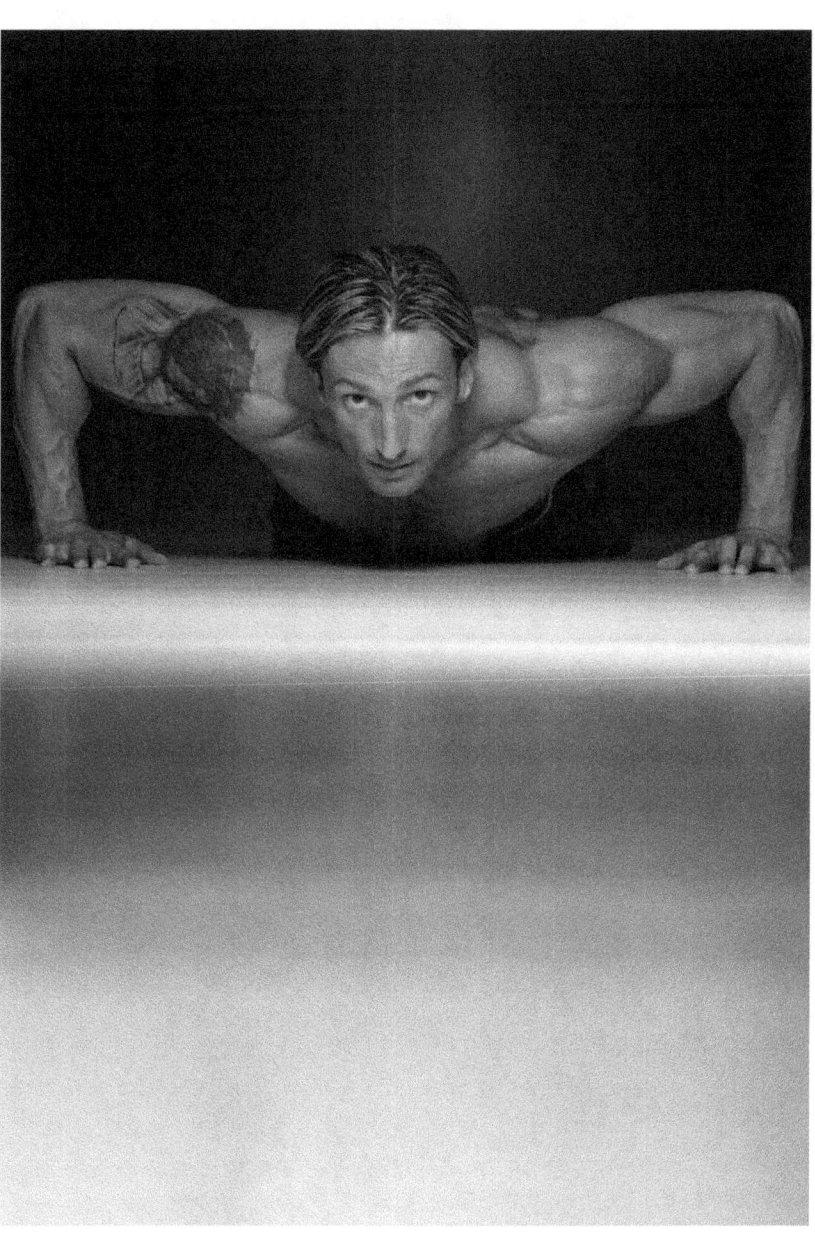

Special Tips for Portraits of Groups

"What I like about photographs is that they capture a moment that's gone forever, impossible to reproduce."

Karl Lagerfeld

Groups cover a lot of shots; it covers everything more than two people. All the way to as big as you can get to fit in the frame.

One easy way to make your group shots more attractive is to not have everyone's head at the same level.

Another way is to create a triangle with the subjects. Triangles are very appealing and will make the shot more interesting.

Here is a nice group shot with all the subjects' heads at different levels. You can see how it makes the shot more interesting and appealing. Make sure you focus on the persons face that is closest to the camera, so they are in focus. In a shot like this if you just let the camera pic the focus spot and it focuses on the man in the back, the girl in the front may be out of focus and it would ruin a great shot.

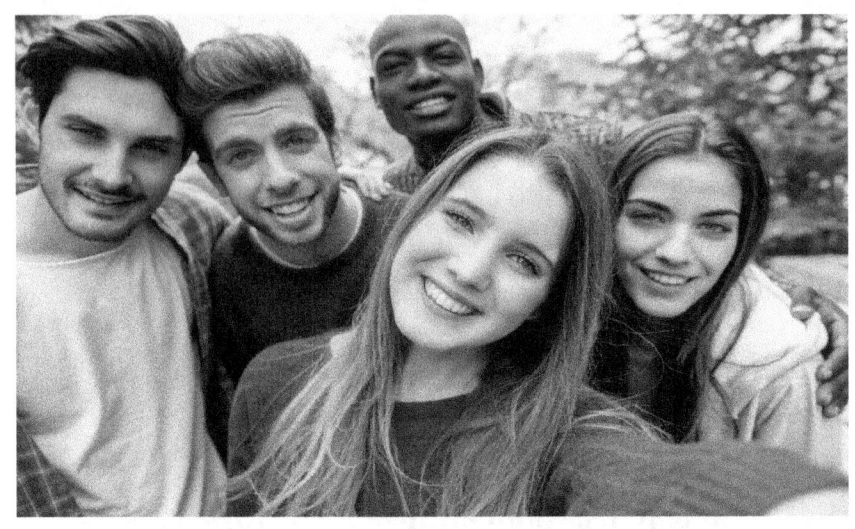

Shoot group photos in a natural setting. Or in a setting that is familiar and comfortable for the subjects is a key to getting great shots. The faster and easier you can get the people in the shot to feel relaxed and at ease, the better the shots will be.

When you are taking family shots, do not forget to get the family pet or pets in the shot of the family, at least some of them. Many people feel their pets are part of their family. And they will likely suggest you get them in the shots. Do not omit them from the shots.

Try different angles; shoot from high and from the sides, and even from low. They may not be the best shots. However, you are going to get some cool shots this way. And with digital cameras, you can delete them if they do not work.

Get everyone in close, turn them so you shoot their body from the sides and get them to look where you want. Getting everyone in tight makes for a warmer and more memorable shot.

If you have time and the opportunity ahead of time. Coordinating clothing can make the shot much better. If all the clothes are neutral or matching, no one person will stand out and everyone will look better. If one of the people is wearing something quite different, it will detract from the shot.

Try to get them to laugh with a funny story or a cheesy joke. Natural smiles always look better than a fake smile. Do not have them say cheese.

Make sure you have enough depth of field to get everyone in focus. Blurring the background is good to do for group shots. If you are not using the location as part of the shot, but you must get all the people in focus.

Have fun with the shots; Have them make some funny faces in some of the shots. If you are having a problem getting any of the group to relax, get them to do some funny poses and take those shots. This will help them relax, and you may get a cool shot or two.

Have the subjects interacting with each other instead of posing. Shoot everything and keep taking photos so you do not miss a great picture. Take all the images you can, one may be a winner.

Always prompt them with positive comments and keep them relaxed and comfortable. The more relaxed they are, the better the shots will be. Talk about how good they look. The colors, and the expressions on their faces, how they relate to the others. The more positive comments you throw at them the better.

If the subjects want traditional family portraits. Do them, but do not stop there, they will get surprised with the other shots you get as well.

Here is a shot that is different. However, it works well because all the parts of the shot are interesting and cool looking. This may not appeal to everyone, but it will to some, and it might be the favorite shot of the day.

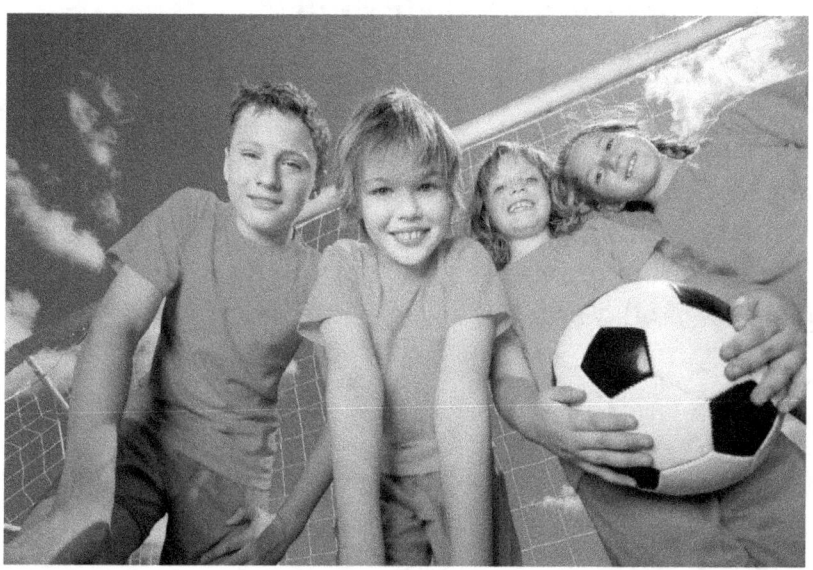

Portraits of Kids

"When you photograph people in color, you photograph their clothes. But when you photograph people in Black and white, you photograph their souls!"

Ted Grant

One of the major things to focus on when doing portraits of kids is to let them be kids. You can shoot traditional kid portraits. However, you get better and more fun shots when you use a longer lens and do candid shots of them doing fun things.

Move around and take lots of shots from different angles and various levels. Get down to their level and take some from a standing position as well.

Lots of times I will put on a longer telephoto lens. Zoom in on them while they are playing and get some fantastic shots.

Here is a neat shot of a little girl playing. It is a candid shot that is a great memory for her and her family for the rest of their lives.

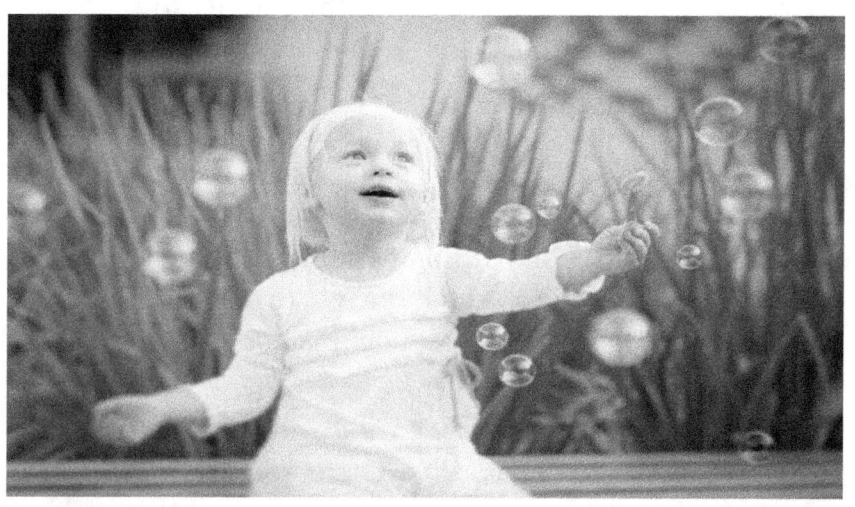

From this shot, you can also see that they do not need to be looking at the camera to get a fantastic shot. They do not even need to know you are taking a picture to get an outstanding photo. If you get them doing something they enjoy doing. They will forget you are even there and act like they will without you there. You will get shots that look like they look when playing, and not posed in any way.

Let them have fun. The worst thing to do is to have a crying kid when you are trying to make a family portrait. It can take a long time to get them happy again if they are crying. Do not let them get to that point. If they are getting restless, or you can see they are getting upset. Change the activity to something fun that they want to do.

When you shoot portraits of babies, many times you must pose them, or have the parent pose them, be ready to get the shot. With kids, you have a short window of opportunity to get the shot. With babies, you have only a second or two to snap it, if you are not prepared, the great shot is gone.

For young babies or kids too small to sit up on their own, you must use props. There are many things you can use as a prop. Something to sit them in or to sit them against to prop them up. Use something that adds to the shot. A stuffed animal or similar prop.

Portraits of Pets

"When people look at my pictures, I want them to feel the way they do when they want to read a line of a poem twice."

— Robert Frank

This shot is not a pet so to speak; it is a zoo shot, but it is one of my favorite portrait shots. Taken at the Como Zoo in St Paul MN. The gorilla is Casey. He has been there for many years. He was very curious when I was there that day. I had to take the shot through glass, and it was rather dark.

I luckily had put my 50mm f1.8 lens on before he did this. He weighs around 450 pounds and is only about 3 feet away from me. I swear he was saying. "How's this?" It is an amazing shot.

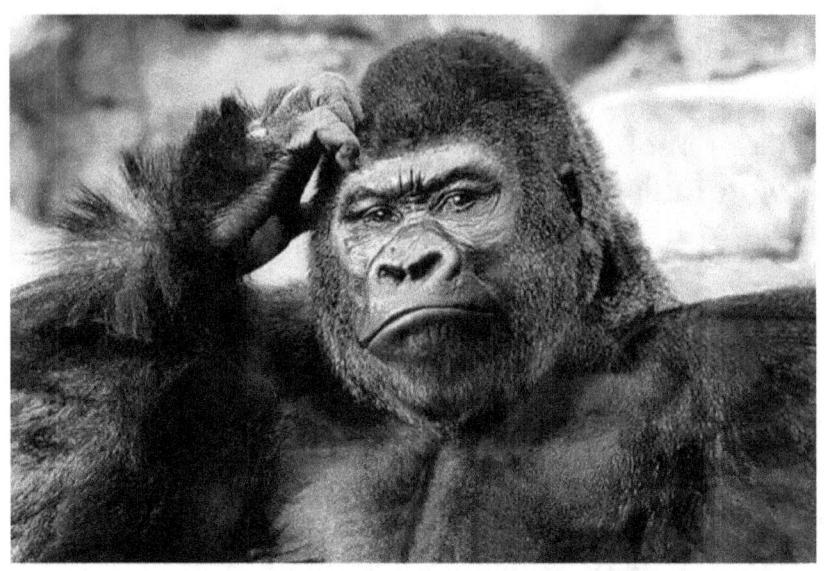

Everyone loves their pets; they are part of our
families. We recently lost a cat that we had as part
of our family for over 15 years. I have taken
hundreds of candid shots of him doing what he did,
never any posed shots, all him doing what he does.

The best pet shots are like the greatest kid shots.
Get action shots when they are doing what they like
to do, and you will get the best shots of them.

Here he is doing one of his favorite things, lying in
the chair on the deck. He loved being outside.

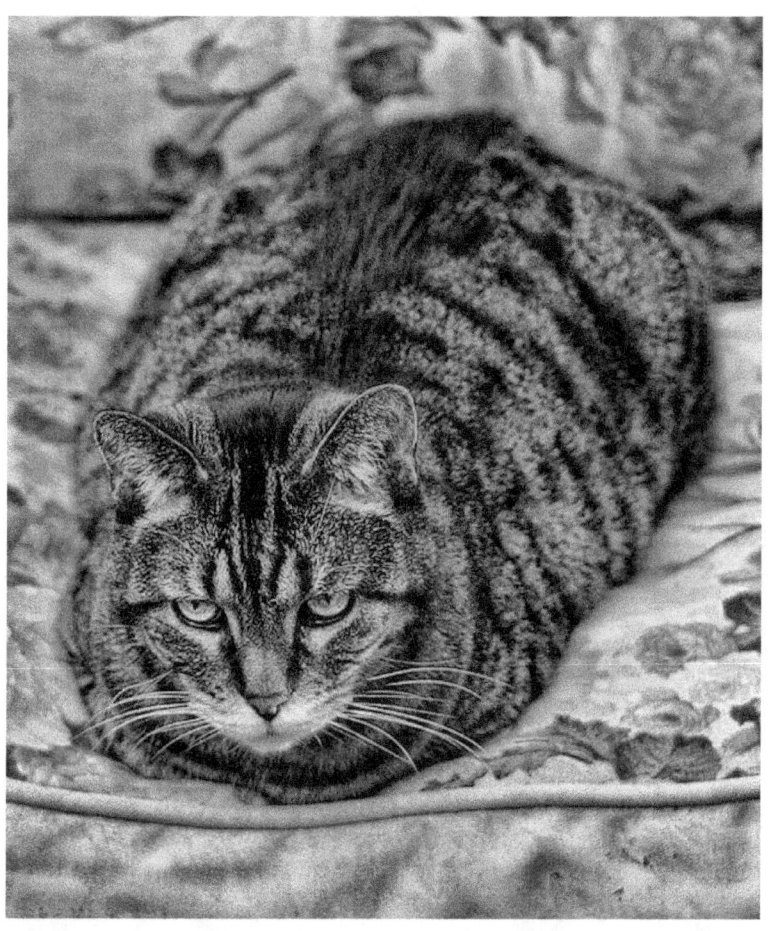

To get great close-up shots of pets. Especially dogs, get them doing something. Get in position and yell their name, when they look, take the shot. I like to have my camera on burst mode when doing that. You will get more shots than you will keep, but you will get better shots as well. They will only look for a second or so, you must be ready.

To get great action shots of your dog, you need to use a fast lens, a high shutter speed, and lots of light.

Another key to great dog shots is to have help. You will need an assistant to get the best dog shots. The assistant should have the dog's toys, and some treats to use to get the dog's' attention. If you must work the toys and the treats while taking the shots, you will miss lots of great shots. The time you have for the shot can be a second or so, be ready all the time.

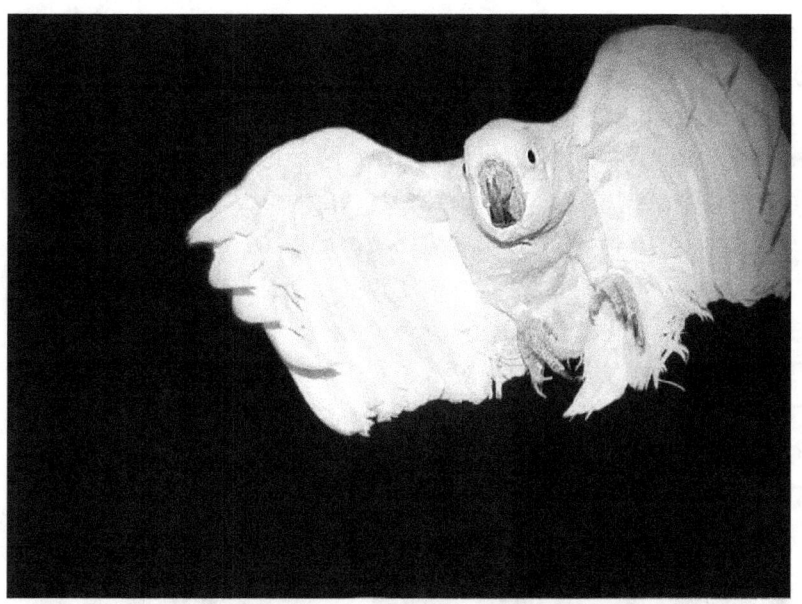

The shot above is another of my favorite pet shots. This is Rocky, our Cockatoo. He loves to fly around the basement and loves to take showers.

I spent several hours getting this shot of him flying and coming into land on his perch. Getting him to fly right and getting the flash and everything else to come together was a job, but it was worth it.

Try to capture the pet's personality when taking the shot. If you can do that, the shot will be far better.

Shooting pet portraits is the same as shooting people portraits when it comes to the basic tips for each. If you are taking a face shot, make sure the eyes are sharp. Use the rule of thirds and the other composition rules as well. Making a great photo takes the same creativity and planning for any type of portrait shot.

If you have a cooperative pet, you can get some great cute shots that are cool. Here is a shot of Rocky posing for me. Cockatoos are great pets, but they are a lot of work.

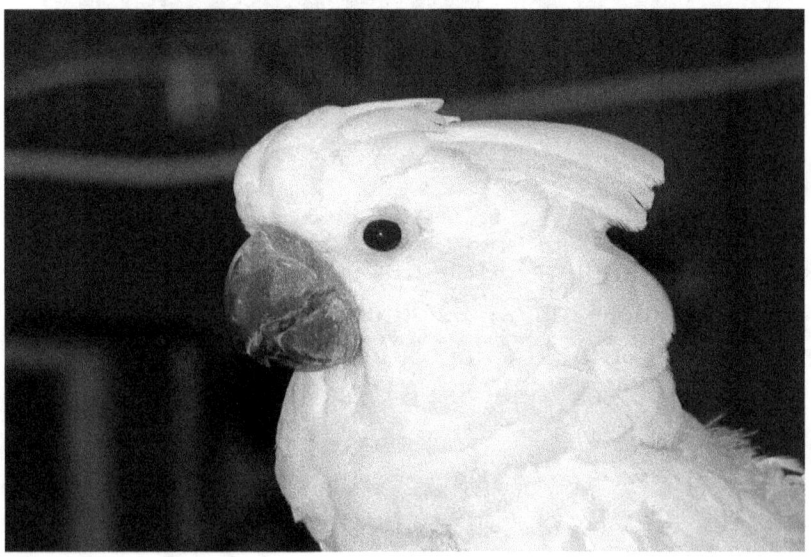

One more pet shot, this is Tiger who passed away a few years ago. He was posing great for this shot.

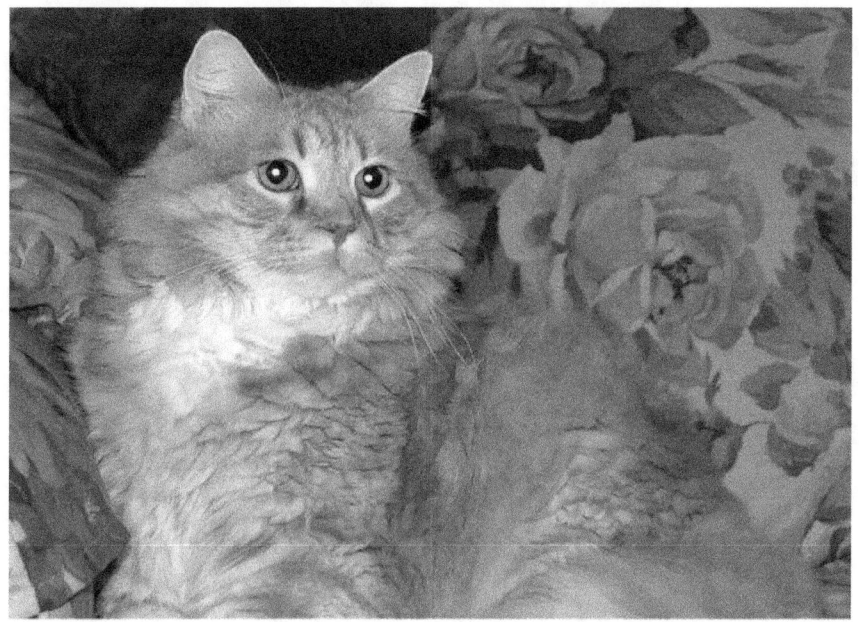

Conclusion

"Your first 10,000 photographs are your worst."

— Henri Cartier-Bresson

Ok, there are a lot of great tips in this book. They are here to show what you can do if you know how to make excellent photos, instead of taking snapshots.

All the tips throughout the book are applicable to every type of portrait shot. For lighting, equipment, and composition, use all the tips for your portrait shooting. Do this and you will make some portraits that will make people say WOW.

I found a cool app that I can carry with me everywhere on my phone or tablet. It is called strike a pose. It has hundreds of poses for all types of portrait shots, and it gives a description of how to do each. The app costs $1.99 from iTunes. I am not associated with this app at all; it is a great resource to have with you all the time.

Keep a swipe file in a place you can access it anytime you need it. This is a key part in getting great portraits. Being able to recreate looks that you like, and the subject will like is important to getting the best portraits you can get.

Think about what the photo is for. If you are shooting for a particular purpose. For instance: A shot for an invitation, a holiday card or something of that nature.

Think about portrait or landscape mode, think about what the people in the shot want out of it, or what you want out of it. Shooting people shots can be challenging but rewarding as well. Have fun and enjoy.

Be careful of the background. Bad backgrounds have ruined many great shots.

If you learned some good tips from this book. I would be very grateful if you could take a minute and **go to the Amazon site and leave a short review.** This will get others to see this book, and will help them be a better photographer.

Thank you for reading my book.

Some other photo books you will enjoy.

Black & White Photography

The art of making great black & white photos

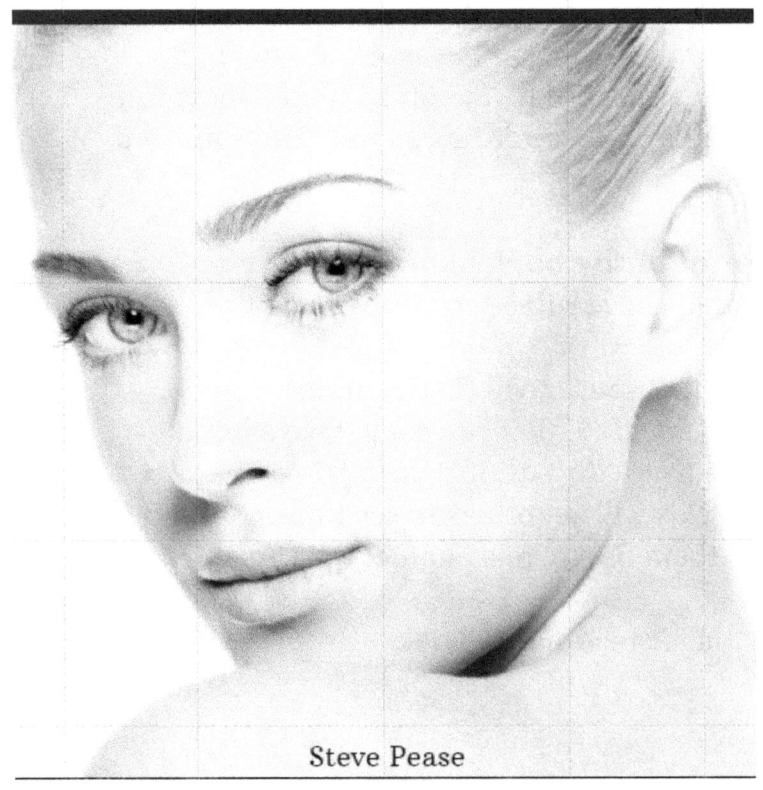

Steve Pease

In this book I will give you tips on how to take the best black and white shots you can. I will show you how to use black and white to change the mood of the shot and create the emotion you want to portray.

I have taken hundreds of thousands of photos over the past 40 years. Many have been black and white. I have studied photography in practice and photography school many years ago. Practice is the best way to learn. Learn by using your eyes and the tools you must make the best shots you can. **Check it out here.**

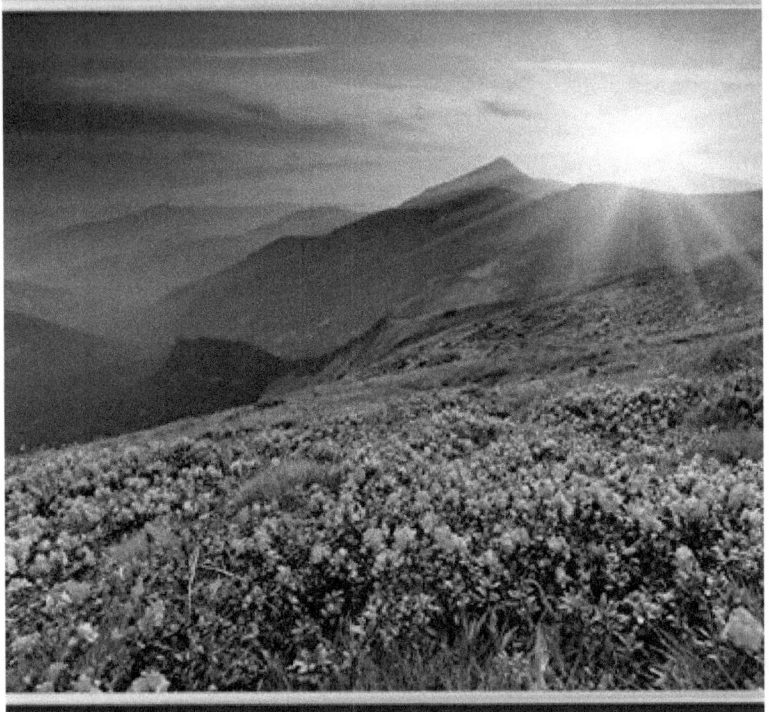

Do you love to make photos?

There is a difference between someone who takes pictures, and someone who makes pictures. Making pictures is all about how you see the parts of the photos you are creating. Practicing the art of taking great pictures is the way to get them to be great. Do you want to learn to be able to make great photos? To be successful you need to practice.

This book is set up with projects for you to do that will help you focus on seeing things the way you need to see them to take great pictures instead of good pictures. Digital photography has become a part of almost everyone's lives, we take pictures all the time, and of everything. We post them on websites and Facebook and send the shots from person to person through text messages. Picture taking has become billions of snapshots. The art of photography is being lost. **Learn to take the best landscapes you can, check it out here.**

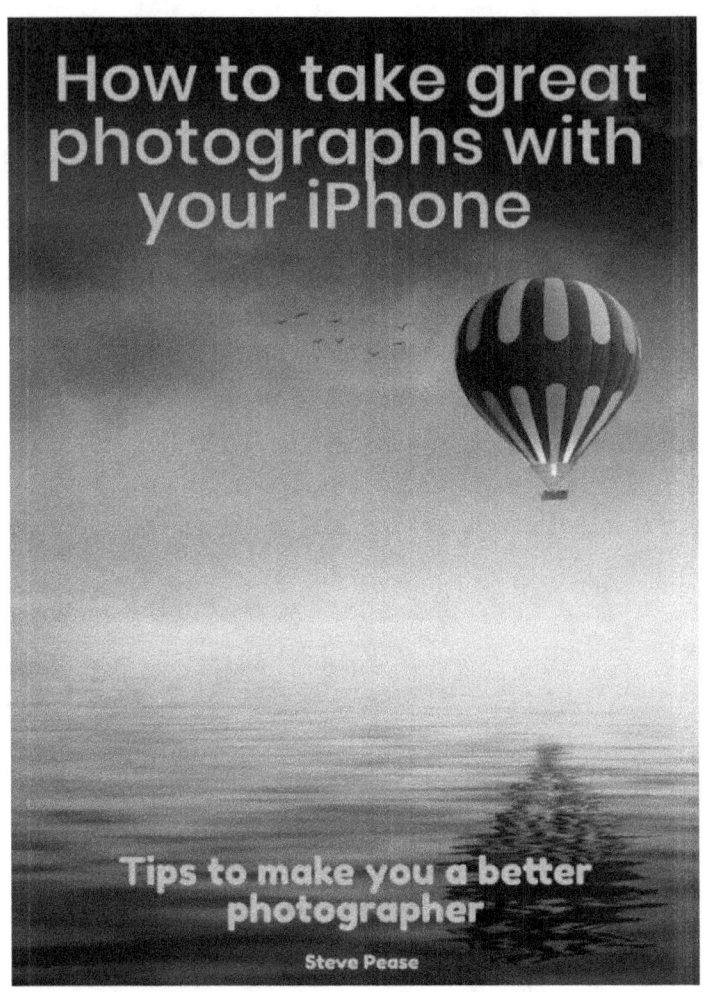

How to take great photographs with your iPhone

Tips to make you a better photographer

Steve Pease

Has this ever happened to you?

You are with your friends and something memorable is happening and you want to capture it so you take some pictures that you will want to keep as memories. You get home and upload them to your computer so you can do some post processing, or just check them out. And maybe you will get some prints made. But your photos are blurry. Not terrible, but not good enough to print.

You got some pictures that you can save for memories on your phone, but they look terrible any bigger. Taking great pictures with a phone camera is harder than with an SLR. A lot of the reason is that the Phone is lighter, which makes it harder to hold still, and you are likely taking those types of pictures while having fun, and not really thinking about taking pictures. **<u>Learn to take the best shots you can with the camera you always have with you.</u>**

Thanks again. Go take great photos.

www.ingramcontent.com/pod-product-compliance
Lightning Source LLC
Chambersburg PA
CBHW070813180526
45168CB00002B/597